MODERN MILITARY AIRCRAFT

Viper
F-16

By Lou Drendel
Color Illustrations by Lou Drendel
1/72 Scale Illustrations by Tom Tullis

squadron/signal publications

If you have any photographs of the aircraft, armor, soldiers or ships of any nation, particularly wartime snapshots, why not share them with us and help make Squadron/Signal's books all the more interesting and complete in the future. Any photograph sent to us will be copied and the original returned. The donor will be fully credited for any photos used. Please send them to:

**Squadron/Signal Publications, Inc.
1115 Crowley Drive.
Carrollton, TX 75011-5010.**

Acknowledgements

General Dynamics	U.S. Air Force
U.S. Navy	Norman E. Taylor
David F. Brown	Ted Carlson
Bobby Armour	Phil Ruhlman
Brian Rogers	Bob Pfannenschmidt
Dave Mason	Roy Chismar
Dimitri Verdoodt	Dick Cole
Paul Hunt	Don Linn
George Cockle	

Foreword

VIPER! Viper? Trust the people who fly them to pick names that will stick with airplanes. "Viper" is the nickname picked by the pilots for the F-16. Its origins go back almost to the drawing board, as does official opposition to the fighters *nom de guerre*. When the name was first advanced within General Dynamics, someone reminded someone else that Viper was also the name of a British jet engine. The Air Force hierarchy was into naming their airplanes after birds of prey just then (F-15 Eagle), and a snake seemed like a come-down...it just didn't have that soaring quality. So was born the official name — Fighting Falcon. It sounds majestic, but just didn't fit into the lexicon of most self-respecting fighter pilots. "Fighting Falcon?" No, that just couldn't be said fast enough, either on the radio or at the bar! "Electric Jet" was a sometimes-used trendy name for the F-16, but since all modern airplanes are fly by wire, it has lost its unique quality. Every fighter pilot, in all U.S. services, refers to his airplane as a "jet" or "the jet," in a kind of studied understatement. But fighter pilots are some of the last great individualists and where individuality is important, the right nickname (or call sign) is of paramount importance. For the F-16, "Viper" seemed just perfect. It is quick and deadly, air-to-air or air-to-ground. But in spite of its popularity with pilots, the name "Viper" remains very much a backroom nickname, rarely, if ever, seen in print...before now.

(Overleaf) The USAF Aerial Demonstration Team, the Thunderbirds, fly F-16s at air shows around the world. The Thunderbirds praise the F-16 as being one of the best demonstration aircraft they have ever flown. (General Dynamics)

The first two General Dynamics YF-16 prototypes carried a flashy Red/White/Blue paint scheme during 1974 as part of the lightweight fighter fly-off. (General Dynamics)

Introduction

It has been more than twenty years since the official birth of the F-16. Back in the sixties, a maverick group of fighter experts were challenging the then-accepted norms of fighter aircraft design. Pierre Sprey, John Boyd and Harry Hillaker came to be known as "The Fighter Mafia" because of their espousal of the lightweight fighter concept.

John Boyd was a former USAF fighter pilot, aeronautical engineer and defense analyst who came to the Pentagon in 1966 to advise the Air Force on its choice for the successor to the F-4. Pierre Sprey was one of McNamara's "whiz kids" who also came to the Pentagon in 1966. Harry Hillaker had worked for General Dynamics as an aircraft designer since the early 1940s. Hillaker's account of the birth of the F-16 was printed in "CODE ONE" the company magazine. Excerpts from that interview are reprinted here with permission from the publishers. Commenting on the "fighter mafia," Hillaker said:

We wanted a change. While most of the Air Force was interested in going north, we wanted to go south. More specifically, they were concerned that we were trying to introduce a new fighter that would jeopardize the F-15. You see, the F-15 was the first air superiority fighter that the Air Force had put under contract in twenty-five years. They were committed to the F-15. They felt strongly that our airplane was just a hot dog airplane that was good only for airshows on sunny Sundays at the state fair. This view was strengthened to a degree by their experience with the Lockheed F-104. The F-104 was a really hot airplane that people loved to fly, but it didn't have much capability and not much range. The Air Force bought only 300 of them.

We were threatening for another reason. We were perceived as being anti-technology. Our slogan was "make it simple." The slogan itself may have been an oversimplification. We didn't articulate ourselves well early on. There have been debates through the years about just how much technology should be incorporated in any design. The real issue isn't technology versus no technology. It is how to apply technology. For example, the F-15 represents a brute-force approach to technology. If you want higher speeds, add bigger engines. If you want longer range, make the airplane bigger to increase fuel capacity. The result is a big airplane. The F-15 was viewed as highly sophisticated because it was so big and expensive. In my mind, the F-15 was not as technically advanced as the F-4.

The F-16 is much more of an application of high technology than the F-15. We used the technology available to drive the given end, that is, or was, to keep things as simple and small as we could. It is a finesse approach. If we wanted to fly faster, we made the drag lower by reducing size and adjusting the configuration itself. If we wanted greater range, we made the plane more efficient, more compact. People tend to focus on one part of a given parameter. You can, for example, get a higher thrust-to-weight ratio by increasing the thrust. You can also get a higher thrust to weight ratio by leaving the thrust alone and reducing the weight, which is what we did on the lightweight fighter.

We had to use this approach because we had to use a given engine, the F-100, which had been developed for the F-15. John Boyd had played a part in defining that engine, and he felt comfortable with it. So the engine was fixed. That meant that the thrust was fixed. If we wanted a high thrust-to-weight ratio, we had no choice but to reduce weight.

The range equation can be treated like the thrust-to-weight ratio. The typical approach to increase range is to simply increase fuel capacity. But increasing fuel capacity increases volume, which means more weight and more drag. People think that big is better. It's not. With the lightweight fighter, we wanted to achieve our ends through different means. We increased range by reducing size.

When I wrote "F-16 Fighting Falcon In Action" in 1982, I commented that the F-16 was the best clear air interceptor in the world at that time. It has since grown to be a very capable all-weather/night interceptor and bomber. This was not what the designers had intended the lightweight fighter to be. They wanted simple and small, and Hillaker said this about that:

In general terms, simple and small translates into lower weight, less drag, and therefore higher performance. Also, a fundamental indicator of an airplane's cost is its weight. We were well aware that the avionics folks would be putting a bunch of gadgets in the airplane, which would increase weight and decrease performance. We stacked the deck. We made the airplane so dense that there wasn't room for all that crap.

As it turned out, that was one of the things that looked as though it might hinder the advancement of the airplane. It was

3

Both prototypes took part in the fly-off competition with the Northrop YF-17, flying a total of 330 missions while the YF-17s flew 268 sorties. The Lightweight Fighter Prototypes never flew against each other, but instead flew against all current USAF fighters plus captured MiG-17s and MiG-21s. (General Dynamics)

The second YF-16 prototype on the ramp at Edwards AFB during May of 1974. The aircraft had been repainted in an Off White/Light Blue experimental camouflage scheme tested during the LWF competition. (USAF)

later graded on the amount of usable space. We had 4.8 cubic feet. The F-15 had almost ten times that.

There was another reason, besides weight, that favored small size. Smaller aircraft have less drag. People always talk in terms of drag coefficients. But drag coefficients really don't tell you that much. For example, the drag coefficient of an F-16 is about the same as that of an F-4; however, the F-16 has about one third the drag of an F-4 in level flight. At angle of attack, it is about one-fifteenth. The airplane's exceptional maneuverability is a consequence of that lower drag and a higher thrust-to-weight ratio.

My first dealings with John Boyd and Pierre Sprey did not involve any airplane designs per se. They were purely and simply an analysis of the relationships of wing loading and thrust loading and fuel fraction (ratio of fuel capacity to the weight of the airplane). We wanted to understand the relationship between these variables. We knew that we wanted low wing loading and high thrust loading. But we also knew that low wing loading meant more weight and more drag. High thrust loading meant high fuel consumption.

Airplanes with high thrust-to-weight ratios are normally equated with short range. That's why we started looking at fuel fractions. We wanted to tie all these things together to get a better feel for the boundaries involved. I would say that people had looked at the problem this way before, but no one had applied it systematically to get a complete picture.

We were trying to determine the trends. We didn't spend a lot of time looking for exact values. It is one thing to agree that something is better. But how much better is another question. The answer involves finding a trend and asking more questions. Is the design being improved by these actions? How fast is it improving for a given amount of change?

The person most responsible for this approach was John Boyd.

Knowing what questions to ask is as important as knowing how to determine the answers. You have to have an innate curiosity. That's what separates the best engineers from the rest. Ask why. Be curious.

The F-16 design approach was different. We usually rush into form before we really understand what the function is. That gets us into trouble. The lightweight fighter brought a new perspective to maximum speed and acceleration. Everyone wanted airplanes to Mach 2 to 2.5. No one asked why.

The fourth full scale development F-16A climbs out from Edwards AFB during the flight test program. It is armed with four AIM-9 Sidewinder air-to-air missiles and an ALQ-119 ECM pod on the centerline pylon. (USAF)

I had the opportunity one time when we were working on the supersonic transport to track all the supersonic flight time on the B-58. We had over one hundred B-58s flying and the most supersonic time on any one airplane was seven hours. Seven hours. This was less than five percent of the total flight time. The entire fleet had a total of 200 hours supersonic. They equated flying top speed with acceleration. Big engine, for those setting the requirements, meant high speed and high acceleration. This is not a true relationship.

With the F-16, we addressed function first. We asked, what value is derived from a given capability? The riskiest portion of our lightweight fighter design was the fly-by-wire system. If the fly-by-wire didn't work, our relaxed static stability wasn't going to work. And then the airplane would have had higher drag and would have been less responsive, less maneuverable. We had a backup that not too many people know about. We designed the fuselage so that if the fly by wire did not work, we could go back to a statically stable design by moving the wing back. We had bulkheads in the fuselage that were designed to carry the load of both placements of the wing.

We weren't the only ones looking at fly by wire. McDonnell Douglas had contracts with the Air Force and the Flight Dynamics Lab for test programs for fly-by-wire systems, relaxed static stability and the high-acceleration cockpit for the F-4. The technology was available, but these companies didn't take advantage of it. Shortly after we won the full-scale development contract for the F-16, I was invited to give a talk to the St. Louis chapter of the American Institute of Aeronautics and Astronautics. My initial response was, "You must be kidding. You want me to go into the lion's den?" McDonnell Douglas did all kinds of advertising and everything else that was anti-lightweight fighter. My immediate reply was, thanks but no thanks.

About fifteen minutes later I got a call from Dave Lewis (then chairman of General Dynamics Corporation). He said, "Harry, I hear that you are giving a talk on the F-16 up here (General Dynamics corporate headquarters was also in St. Louis.) to these McAir guys. That's great! I want you to give them hell, and I'm going to be there to see you do it."

I called the AIAA guy back up and said I've had second thoughts. A presentation might be fun. I didn't really think that. But I'm influenced by politics too. A couple of days before the meeting the program chairman said that the chapter had sold more tickets to that meeting than any other past meeting, even meetings with astronaut speakers. He said they had over one hundred coming from McDonnell Douglas alone. You can imagine how I felt.

I gave the talk. After about an hour of questions and answers, the program chairman interrupted to let those who wanted to leave, leave. Two hours after that, the hotel manager came in the room and asked us to leave because they had to set up the room for a breakfast the next morning. At 2:30 in the morning, about fifteen McAir guys and I closed the bar. These were the same people who worked on fly by wire, relaxed static stability and the high-acceleration cockpit, all the test programs the Air Force and its Flight Dynamics Laboratory had conducted for the F-4, which McDonnell had the contract for.

Now here's McDonnell building the F-15, the world's latest-greatest fighter, which did not contain one of these technologies. I had 125 McDonnell guys who were more interested in the F-16 than they were in their own F-15 because they saw the fruits of their labors being incorporated in my airplane. They did not incorporate these technologies because the F-15 was very expensive. It had been twenty-five years since the Air Force had had an air superiority fighter. It had taken more than five years just to get the program approved. They couldn't afford to take any risks. On the other hand, the contract for the lightweight fighter prototype was for a best effort. We did not have to deliver an airplane, legally. Once we spent our $37 million, we could have piled all the parts on a flatbed trailer and said to Mr. Air Force, here's your airplane. We could fly the airplane when we were ready to fly the airplane.

We pushed for a flyable airplane because we were competing against Northrop. But my point is that we were not working

The first full scale development F-16A carried a special paint scheme with the flags of the four European co-production partners (plus the French flag representing a visit to the Paris air show) on the nose. The French had the F-16's principle rival for foreign orders, the Mirage F-1. (General Dynamics)

against a difficult, but arbitrary, schedule. And I think most schedules are arbitrary. Furthermore, there was no fixed follow-on. The airplane was simply a technology demonstrator.

Northrop was also unwilling to take risks with their prototype because they wanted an airplane to replace their F-5. They were more interested in sales to foreign markets and stayed very rigid and conservative in their design because they wanted to be able to show their foreign markets the airplane at any point in its design. We were interested in what the U.S. Air Force wanted, and we stayed flexible in the design to respond to their needs. We looked at a number of designs. We waited until the very last to choose the best one. We could afford to put these advanced technologies into the airplane. We were more apt to accept the risk.

A number of companies were caught off guard by our winning the lightweight fighter prototype contract. They were out there promoting their ideas around the Air Force. We weren't. We were deliberately quiet about what we were doing because we were handicapped with a bad reputation, though quite undeserved, from the F-111 days. We couldn't brag. Instead, we quietly did our homework and did it thoroughly.

We were ready to fly the lightweight prototype on 1 February 1974. We found out Northrop wasn't flying until June or July. That really worried us. We first thought that they had one-upped us. Their design is a production design, we thought, not a prototype. In actuality, they were just behind. One of the reasons the Air Force eventually chose our design was that it was closer to a full-scale development than Northrop's.

As the F-16 metamorphosed from ideas to reality, Sprey and Boyd admonished Hillaker for diverging from the purity of their original concept of "keep it simple." Hillaker replied:

If we had stayed with the original lightweight fighter concept, that is, a simple day fighter, we would have produced only 300 F-16s, the same number of F-104s that were built. This is not to say that their complaints are unreasonable. When you load up an F-16 with external fuel tanks, bombs and an electronic countermeasures pod on the centerline, you've doubled its drag. For someone who's worked all his life to achieve minimum drag, that's sacrilegious. Nonetheless, it speaks well for the airplane.

There's no question that ninety to ninety-five percent of the design of the F-16 was based on the European scenario. We may have understood requirements for Middle East and Far East scenarios, but those scenarios were completely masked by the European theater. In fact, every aircraft we have in inventory and every one we have under development is driven by the European scenario.

The F-16 has far exceeded my expectations. However, if I had realized at the time that the airplane would have been used as a multi-mission, primarily an air-to-surface airplane as it is used now, I would have designed it differently. The F-16XL had a better balance of air-to-air and air-to-ground capability. In fact, when I first started going to the Air Force with plans for the F-16XL, some of the Air Force people were so enthusiastic about it that they accused me of holding the design back so that we could sell the airplane twice. If you know anything about the history of the lightweight fighter, you know this was not the case.

With the F-16XL, we reduced the drag of the weapon carriage by sixty-three percent. The drag of the XL with the same fuel and twice as many bombs is a little over thirty percent less than today's F-16 when you load it up. We could never make the grade on the F-16XL because the improvements on range and cruise speed were unnecessary for the European scenario. The F-16 as loaded up and as high drag as it gets can still handle the distances involved in Europe. This is not necessarily the case in the Middle East, and even less so in Southeast Asia. I'm not sure if this situation will change because the only place the problem shows up is in lack of range.

The cockpit of the F-16 shows the influence of modern electronics in the cockpit layout, with principle flight instrument displayed on the HUD and the backup pressure instruments occupying a decidedly secondary position at the bottom of the instrument panel. (General Dynamics)

The range of the F-16 would play a factor in the Gulf War of 1991, though the strategy and tactics of that air war resulted in a quick victory which minimized any range problems. But that was after nearly twenty years of F-16 history.

The F-16A used the Aces II ejection seat. The 30 degree rearward tilt gives the pilot additional G tolerance by changing the vector of blood draining from the pilot's head during high G maneuvering. (Dave Mason)

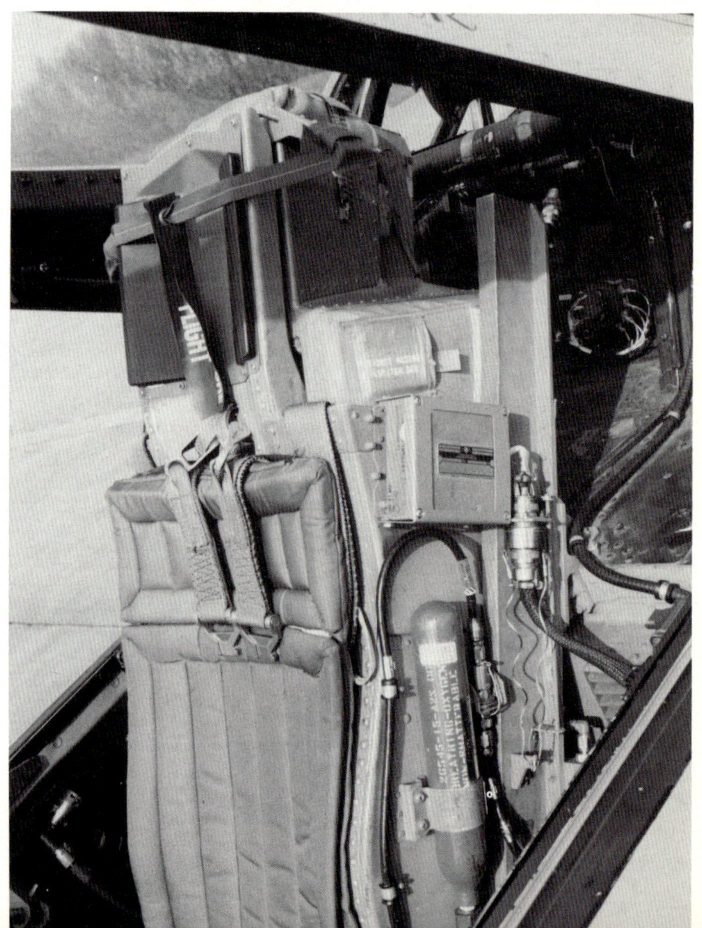

F-16 Almanac

August, 1972 - General Dynamics and Northrop are selected by the USAF to build lightweight fighter prototypes, one of which will be chosen for production.

13 December 1973 - The first of two YF-16 prototypes was rolled out of the General Dynamics plant in Fort Worth, Texas.

20 January 1974 - The first YF-16 made an unexpected first flight at Edwards AFB. Company test pilot Phil Oestricher encountered severe oscillations during high speed ground tests. When the tail scraped on the runway as the nose was raised, he decided to take off and regain control in the air. The flight lasted six minutes and ended uneventfully. The scheduled first flight of 22 January was delayed until a new right stabilator could be installed.

2 February 1974 - The number one YF-16 made its first full flight, with company test pilot Phil Oestricher at the controls. The prototype lightweight fighter reached 400 mph and 30,000 feet.

3 June 1974 - YF-16 prototypes are returned to flight status after an eleven day suspension of testing to correct a problem with the fuel control of the Pratt & Whitney F-100 engine, which caused the engine to go to uncommanded idle in flight, causing two dead-stick landings.

9 September 1974 - The Navy announced that it would select a single contractor to begin engineering development of its VFAX strike fighter. The light strike fighter would be selected from seven proposals, including a Naval version of the YF-16.

October 1974 - Defense Secretary James R. Schlesinger announced that he was considering production of both YF-16 and YF-17 prototypes to satisfy USAF, Navy and export requirements. Meanwhile, congress continued to push hard for production of a single aircraft to satisfy all requirements, apparently having learned nothing from the F-111 program.

October 1974 - Two members of the Dutch parliamentary military affairs committee alleged that they had been approached with bribe offers from a representative of Avions Marcel Dassault-Breguet Aviation. The charges, which were denied by Dassault, were made in connection with a possible Dutch order for Mirage F-1 fighters. Belgian, Dutch, Danish, and Norwegian defense ministers met in Brussels to review proposals for a new fighter aircraft to replace their F-104G Starfighters.

October 1974 - After completion of Air Combat testing, company test pilots Phil Oestricher and Neal Anderson said that the YF-16's ability to sustain high G loads and maneuver in the vertical would revolutionize air combat. They claimed that the YF-16 could out-maneuver any current fighter. The USAF announced that the production configurations of both prototype lightweight fighters would be changed to accommodate a larger radar antenna.

13 January 1975 - Air Force Secretary John L. McLucas announced the F-16 as the winner of the USAF lightweight fighter competition, with plans to purchase 650 aircraft. The initial fixed price incentive contract was for fifteen engineering development versions of the F-16, eleven single seat F-16As and four two seat F-16Bs, at a cost of $417.9 million. The Navy said that it was leaning towards a re-engined version of the F-16 for its strike fighter. The battle for the export version of the lightweight fighter continued, although it was acknowledged that General Dynamics now had the inside track to beat Northrop (F-17) and Dassault (Mirage F-1).

February 1975 - The NATO consortium was offered the F-16 at a unit flyaway price of $5.16 million in 1975 dollars. This price was based on a total production run of 2,000 aircraft, including USAF, NATO and third country orders. The U.S. Government cleared F-100 engine technology transfer to these countries.

March 1975 - In a demonstration of the YF-16s agility, LCOL James G. Rider, director of the F-16 air combat fighter joint test force, outclimbed and out-turned an F-4E by wide margins at Edwards AFB. The USAF announced that it would evaluate four BD-5J light jets as possible transition trainers for the F-16. Bede quoted an out-the-door price of $29,000 each for the BD-5Js.

The F-16XL was a follow-on development of the F-16A intended for the ground attack role. The cranked arrow design wing enabled the F-16XL to carry much greater loads at long range. The aircraft's first flight was on 29 October 1982 with company test pilots Alex Wolfe and Jim McKinney aboard. (General Dynamics)

A single-seat version of the F-16XL was also built and tested. The F-16XL design competed with the F-15E Strike Eagle for the USAF contract for a long-range deep interdiction fighter. The contract was won by the F-15E. (General Dynamics)

The AFTI F-16 was developed following General Dynamics' success with the CCV YF-16. The AFTI version featured a digital flight control system, movable canard flight control surfaces (tested on the CCV) and a dorsal spine with additional avionics. The aircraft was used for numerous test programs which included helmet-aimed weapons, voice activated systems and advanced LANTIRN. (General Dynamics)

The F-16 family arranged for a family portrait. From top to bottom: F-16 AFTI, F-16/79, F-16C, F-16A and F-16XL. Only the F-16A and F-16C actually made it into full scale production and service use. (General Dynamics)

May 1975 - The YF-16 made its first transatlantic flight for a sales demonstration tour to NATO countries, including an appearance at the Paris Air Show.

June 1975 - Belgium, Denmark, Norway and the Netherlands announced plans to purchase 348 F-16s. A coproduction agreement between the four NATO nations and the U.S. called for assembly lines in Belgium and the Netherlands to produce the aircraft, beginning in 1976.

August 1975 - Manufacture of the first F-16 begins in the General Dynamics Fort Worth plant which also produced B-24s, B-36s, B-58s and F-111s. NASA announced that it had conducted free flight wind tunnel tests of vertical-takeoff-and-landing (VTOL) versions of both the F-16 and F-17 at its Langley Research Center.

December 1975 - Assembly of the first F-16A began at General Dynamics Fort Worth plant.

July 1976 - The first European co-production contract was signed.

October 1976 - The first production F-16A was rolled out.

December 1976 - First flight of the F-16A.

January 1977 - The USAF announced plans to purchase an additional 738 F-16s.

May 1977 - An F-16 flew non-stop, unrefueled, across the United States.

July 1977 - The USAF revealed results of testing of one of the YF-16 prototypes as a Control Configured Vehicle. The CCV YF-16 was modified with eight square foot canards on each side of the fuselage inlet. An auxiliary flight control computer augmented the digital computer which controlled the fly-by-wire control system. The CCV F-16 demonstrated flat turns, lateral fuselage pointing, lateral translation mode, nose point down and vertical translation mode. These unconventional movements were most effective during air combat maneuvering.

8 August 1977 - The first F-16B made its first flight with company test pilots Neil Anderson and Phil Oestricher at the controls. It reached 30,000 feet and Mach 1.2.

October 1977 - DOD authorized full-scale F-16 production.

November 1977 - F-16A test aircraft fired AIM-7F Sparrow AAMs.

February 1978 - The first European F-16 assembly line opened at SONACA/SABCA in Belgium.

April 1978 - General Dynamics revealed that it had tested the two seat F-16B in the Wild Weasel role. The company funded project included antenna pods on the wingtips in place of AIM-9 missiles, integration of systems to fire Shrike and Standard ARM radar homing missiles and Maverick AGMs. The first European F-16 was nearing completion at the Fokker-VFW plant at Schiphol in the Netherlands. The final assembly plant at Schiphol covered 58,000 square feet.

17 May 1978 - General Dynamics announced completion of a 16,000 hour equivalent test on an F-16 airframe in a computer-controlled test apparatus at Fort Worth. The test took a year to complete and identified areas of the airframe most susceptible to fatigue. Over 100 computer-directed hydraulic pressure rams were applied to the airframe to simulate in-flight stresses of up to 10 Gs.

May 1978 - The GAO urged Defense Secretary Harold Brown to require a complete review of the F-16 program, citing changed threats when production of the F-16 was scheduled to end in 1987. The USAF replied that the F-16 demonstrated survivability equal to or superior to current aircraft flying similar missions.

June 1978 - The USAF announced adoption of three tone Gray camouflage for production F-16s. This scheme was also adopted by Belgium.

7 August 1978 - Test pilot Neil Anderson flew the first flight of the number one production F-16A. Delivery of the first F-16 was made later in the month to the 388th TFW at Hill AFB, Utah. The Imperial Iranian Air Force announced plans to acquire 160 F-16s, and congress approved the sale of seventy-five F-16s to Israel. The developmental F-16s passed the 2,600 flight hours milestone.

31 October 1978 - First flight of a USAF F-16 with European-made wings.

30 November 1978 - Hill AFB, Utah is designated as the world-wide F-16 system logistical center.

11 December 1978 - First flight of the first European F-16, flown by Belgian test pilot Serge Martin of SABCA, with Neil Anderson riding in the rear seat of the F-16B. YF-16 prototype demonstrated the ability to score hits consistently on a 24 square foot target with laser guided bombs, using a Martin Marietta Automatic Tracking Laser Illumination Pod attached to the lower right side of the inlet duct.

6 January 1979 - Official delivery of the first production F-16A to the 388th TFW at Hill AFB, Utah. The USAF and European F-16 pilots received their initial training from the 388th Wing.

26 January 1979 - In ceremonies at Gosselies, Belgium, the Belgian Air Force received its first F-16, an F-16B, which was to be the first of 116 for the BAF. F-16s passed the 3865 flight hours milestone.

3 May 1979 - The first F-16 for the Royal Netherlands Air Force made its first flight with test pilot Henk Temmen at the controls. It was the first of 174 F-16s to be produced by Fokker-VFW.

6 June 1979 - In ceremonies at Amsterdam, the first Dutch F-16 was turned over to the RNLAF. 90 F-16s were scheduled for delivery during 1979. F-16s passed the 5,300 flight hours milestone. Also in June - Pentagon officials stated that policies of the Carter White House and State Department had cost the U.S. and the European consortium sales of up to 140 export fighters. Countries which expressed interest in the F-16 but were rebuffed by the Carter administration included Jordan, Taiwan, and South Korea.

10 August 1979 - After orientation flights in the F-16, USAF Chief of Staff GEN Lew Allen, Jr. and TAC commander GEN W.L. Creech praised the new fighter as "first class" and "a pilot's airplane." LTGEN Marcel DeSmet, Chief of Staff of the Belgian Air Force quickly won dogfights against two F-104s on his first flight in the F-16, pronouncing it the best of the 60 different types of aircraft he had flown in his career. F-16s passed the 6,500 flight hour milestone.

November 1979 - General Dynamics announced a company-funded development project to mate the General Electric J-79 engine with the F-16 airframe to produce a cheaper export version of the F-16. The unit flyaway cost was expected to be $1 million less than a standard F-16A.

January 1980 - The first F-16s were delivered to Israel, Denmark and Norway. The Israeli F-16s incorporated seventeen engineering changes from the USAF version, primarily to the computer software to accommodate several weapons which were peculiar to the IAF inventory. Other changes were to the navigation and communications equipment.

February 1980 - General Dynamics announced that testing and deliveries of the F-16 were well ahead of schedule. Daily sortie rates from Hill AFB were thirty-eight percent above projections. Similar rates were reported by the European air forces flying the F-16.

March 1980 - The Dutch government announced plans to increase its F-16 order from 102 to 213 aircraft. The USAF delivered an F-16 to General Dynamics for modification as the Advanced Fighter Technology Integration (AFTI) Program demonstrator.

May 1980 - The Dutch minority party urged its government to forsake the European co-production agreement on F-16s, claiming that a direct buy of the aircraft from General Dynamics would save $200 million, which the Dutch could then use to develop the Fokker F-29 short haul transport.

An F-16A of the 6510th Test Wing, Edwards AFB, California carries a Norwegian NFT Penguin anti-ship missile on the outboard pylon. The Penguin has a range of 22 to 24 miles at low altitude and its launch envelope includes speeds up to .95 Mach, 60 degree dive and 4 G turn. (General Dynamics)

The #2 F-16B has been the test-bed for several advanced systems, including close air support (CAS) refinements such as a head-steered FLIR (Forward Looking Infrared) also known as the *Falcon Eye* (just forward of the canopy). The aircraft carries the European One camouflage of two tone Green and Gunship Gray for these tests. (General Dynamics)

The first Block 40 F-16C was given a special paint scheme to highlight the night/all-weather bomber role. The improvements included APG-68(V) radar, Martin Marietta LANTIRN, four channel digital flight control system, expanded computer memory, diffractive optics HUD, improved leading edge slats, stronger landing gear and provisions for advanced EW and IFF equipment. Deliveries began in December of 1988. (General Dynamics)

An F-16B of the 6510th Test Wing was used as the chase aircraft for the B-2 Stealth bomber during its flight tests at Edwards AFB. The F-16s assigned to the test wing carry a high visibility Red and White paint scheme. (USAF)

Agile Falcon was a redesign of the basic F-16 which incorporated a larger wing and additional stores-carrying capabilities. The USAF and the original four European co-development partners shared preliminary developmental funding to evolve the concept with the program starting during 1989. (General Dynamics)

The Lockheed YF-22 was the winner of the Advanced Tactical Fighter contract. The YF-22 prototype is flanked by the two current USAF fighters, the F-15 Eagle and the F-16 Fighting Falcon. (General Dynamics)

June 1980 - U.S. Defense Department formally offered Egypt forty F-16s, along with weapons, spare engines and support equipment worth $961.1 million under the project "Peace Vector."

July 1980 - The USAF officially named the F-16 "Fighting Falcon." The Israeli Air Force accepted its first four F-16s in Israel, following an eleven hour, 6,000 mile ferry flight from Pease AFB, New Hampshire. General Dynamics unveiled plans to build a Mach 2.2 F-16, under the designation F-16XL Scamp. The new design featured a cranked arrow wing attached to a stretched F-16 fuselage. The F-16XL was projected to have supersonic cruise, 125% increase in mission radius, 33% less takeoff and landing distance, higher sea level penetration speeds with more payload and better maneuverability. McDonnell Douglas announced that its close support version of the F-15 would attend the Farnborough Air Show in England. (This would become the F-15E, the principle rival of the F-16XL for a USAF contract for an all-weather penetration fighter.)

August 1980 - Within the space of a week, the Carter Defense Department favored increased F-16 production over the F-15, then questioned the combat capability of the F-16, which was scheduled to replace the F-4 in USAFE.

11 September 1980 - In a demonstration staged for visiting Austrian Air Force officials, the F-16 showed its ability as a point defense interceptor. A two seat F-16B took off from Fort Worth 116 seconds after engine start, climbed to 40,000 feet and accelerated to Mach 2 within six minutes of brake release.

29 October 1980 - The prototype F-16/79 made its first flight from Fort Worth with company test pilot James A. McKinney at the controls. General Dynamics received approval from the U.S. Government to brief 20 countries on the the F-16/79. General Electric announced a new version of the J-79, the J-79-GE-17X, which could be boosted to 18,730 lbst in afterburner.

December 1980 - First flight of the F-16/101 development aircraft. The new General Electric F-101 engine was installed in the first of eight full-scale development F-16s. F-16s pass the 60,000 flight hours mark.

January 1981 - 349 Squadron of the Belgian Air Force became the first F-16 fighter squadron assigned to NATO. The F-16/79 completed the development flight test program.

February 1981 - An evaluation team from the Venezuelan Air Force (FAV) flew the F-16/79 prototype at Fort Worth. The first F-16 refueling from a KC-10 and the first firing of the Advanced Medium Range Air-to-Air Missile (AMRAAM) from an F-16 also occurred.

March 1981 - The 100th F-16 produced in Europe was delivered to the Royal Netherlands Air Force. Twelve F-16s of the 388th TFW returned to Hill AFB, Utah, from Norway, after completing the USAF's first F-16 overseas deployment. The USAF announced that it would develop a new advanced tactical fighter, with a target date of 1985 for design selection. The F-16XL was announced as a prime candidate.

May 1981 - The 400th F-16 was delivered to Hill AF and assigned to the 474th TFW. The USAF announced that completion of the eighteen month F-16 Multinational Operational Test and Evaluation Program (MOT&E) showed that the F-16 exceeded expectations in air-to-air and air-to-ground roles. The MOT&E team operated for six weeks at each of four European air bases. This followed over a year of testing in the United States.

7 June 1981 - F-16s of the Israeli Air Force successfully attacked a nearly completed Iraqi nuclear reactor near Baghdad, using 2,000 pound Mk 84 bombs to destroy the target. A U.S. DOD official said of the attack, "You can't help but admire their technical proficiency, although we strongly condemn the action." President Reagan reacted by delaying shipment of four F-16s due for delivery to Israel.

June 1981 - A team of seven F-16s from Hill AFB won a joint Royal Air Force-USAF bombing competition held at RAF Lossiemouth, Scotland. The F-16s competed against RAF Jaguars and Buccaneers and USAF F-111s in the bombing competition and defended themselves against RAF Lightnings and F-4s. The F-16s achieved eighty-eight kills, without a single loss. The first F-16s to be based overseas arrived at Kunsan AB, Korea as part of the 8th TFW Wolfpack. The F-16s replaced F-4 Phantoms.

This F-16A (81-0777) was used by several units. Initially it was assigned to the 4th Tactical Fighter Squadron, 388th Tactical Fighter Wing at Hill Air Force Base, Utah during June of 1985. (Brian Rogers)

July 1981 - The USAF awarded General Dynamics a $15.9 million contract for study and design during initial work on the F-16 capability enhancement program. Included in this work was qualification of the F-16 for LANTIRN. The Belgian Air Force announced that its F-16 fighters had averaged an 88% in-service rate during the first two years of their operation.

August 1981 - F-16s were grounded following a fatal crash at Hill AFB. Modification kits were installed in F-16s to correct a problem with the bleed air valve on the 13th stage of the F-16s F-100 engine. When the bleed air valve stuck open, bleed air was directed onto the emergency power unit, causing an electrical surge which shut down the flight control computer and caused an uncommanded pitch over. Installation of the kits and restoration to flight status was accomplished within two weeks. The Reagan Administration lifted the embargo on F-16 shipments to Israel. An F-16 destroyed a QF-102 drone in the first guided launch of the AMRAAM.

September 1981 - The 500th F-16 rolled off the assembly line at Fort Worth. The U.S. Government approved the sale of forty F-16s to Egypt, and Congress was notified of intent to sell thirty-six F-16s to South Korea. F-16s passed the 90,000 flight hour mark. USAF LCOL R. Dean Stickell, Commander of the 16th TFS, became the first pilot to log 1,000 hours in the F-16. The first F-16s for the 50th TFW at Hahn AB arrived in Germany.

October 1981 - The USAF accepted the seventy-fifth F-16 for the Israeli Air Force, completing the first foreign military sale of the F-16. The first F-16 for Pakistan was flight tested at Fort Worth. The Reagan Administration agreed to the sale of twenty-four F-16s to Venezuela at a total cost of $600 million.

December 1981 - Pakistan and South Korea formally signed letters of intent to purchase F-16s.

January 1982 - The Egyptian Air Force accepted its first six F-16s at Fort Worth, twenty-three months after signing the letter of agreement between U.S. and Egyptian governments. The Hughes AIM-120 AMRAAM was selected for development over a competing design by Raytheon. The Belgian government agreed to provide $5.9 million to cover the cost of long-lead production items for a possible follow-on sale of F-16s. The money came out of the budget for replacement of Belgium's Mirage 5s.

February 1982 - For static firing tests at Fort Worth, a GPU-5/A (GEPOD-30) four-barrel 30MM gun pod was mounted on the centerline of an F-16A. 500 rounds were fired by remote control in a prelude to flight tests at Edwards AFB.

March 1982 - Egypt accepted the first six of its forty F-16s in country. The USAF announced that Air National Guard and Air Force Reserve units would be equipped with the F-16. The USAF announced that its flight demonstration team, the Thunderbirds, would trade in their T-38s for F-16s. F-16s went the 100,000 flight hour mark.

May 1982 - Congress was notified that Egypt had signed an order for forty additional F-16s. Venezuela signed an order for twenty-four F-16s.

June 1982 - The 200th F-16 assembled in Europe was delivered. Production was equally divided between Fokker and SONACA/SABCA.

July 1982 - The AFTI (Advanced Fighter Technology Integration) F-16 was flown for the first time. The F-16XL made its first flight, with company test pilot Jim McKinney at the controls, two days after being rolled out of the General Dynamics plant at Fort Worth.

October 1982 - The first flight of the number two F-16XL, a two seater powered by the General Electric F-101 prototype engine, was made by company test pilots Alex Wolfe and Jim McKinney. Pakistan accepted the first of its F-16s.

November 1982 - Transition of the Thunderbirds from the T-38 to the F-16 was completed. The first Thunderbird F-16 team was led by MAJ James D. Latham, who had previously flown right wing on the team between 1978 and 1980.

January 1983 - The USAF F-16 tested a Texas Instruments FLIR (Forward looking infrared) system pod during a night mission as a prelude to full-scale testing of the Martin Marietta Lantirn system.

February 1983 - Luke AFB, Arizona was activated as a major F-16 training base. Belgium agreed to purchase an additional forty-four F-16s.

April 1983 - The second USAFE F-16 wing was activated at Torrejon AB, Spain. The Thunderbirds flew their first public F-16 demonstration.

July 1983 - The 1,000th F-16 was delivered to Hill AFB. The first Air National Guard F-16 base was activated at McEntire ANGB, S.C.

September 1983 - Venezuela accepted its first F-16s. Turkey announced its decision to purchase 160 F-16s.

October 1983 - F-16 units placed 1st, 2nd and 4th in USAF-wide gunnery and bombing competition, Gunsmoke 83

November 1983 - The first F-16 was delivered to Venezuela.

December 1983 - The Dutch parliament approved purchase of an additional fifty-seven F-16s, bringing their total to 213. Funding for an additional seventy-five F-16s for Israel was approved.

January 1984 - The first Air Force Reserve F-16 base was activated at Hill AFB, Utah. General Dynamics awarded a contract to Bendix Flight Systems for a new quadruple-redundant digital fly-by-wire flight control system for the forthcoming F-16C/D versions of the Viper.

February 1984 - The USAF Aeronautical Systems Division announced that it was studying incorporation of an integrated avionics system in the F-16. Project Pave Pillar was the USAF initiative to develop the integrated avionics system for the projected advanced tactical fighter. The USAF projected a 67% improvement in cumulative sorties on target with use of Pave Pillar. Using Pave Pillar in the F-16 was projected to result in a 90% reduction in cables and connectors, improvement of mean time between failures of avionics from

7.3 hours to 35 hours, and a reduction of maintenance man hours for avionics from 17% to 5% of total maintenance man hours.

19 June 1984 - First flight of the F-16C.

July 1984 - The first F-16C was delivered to the Air Force. The F-16C was announced as a contender for fighter selection by Greece. The AFTI F-16 was modified with an automated maneuvering attack system for the second phase of the AFTI/F-16 program at NASA's Ames-Dryden facility.

August 1984 - Denmark ordered twelve additional F-16s after delivery of its first fifty-eight were completed.

November 1984 - Flight testing of the new F-16C revealed problems associated with software difficulties, cracking of ventral fins due to turbulence caused by lantirn pods, ECS shutdowns, and flaperon cracks. Dain M. Hancock, program director of the F-16 Multinational Staged Improvement Plan Program, stated that, "Development lead times that were once paced by hardware are becoming paced by software." He noted that one of the problems facing aircraft manufacturers was a shortage of people who understood both computers and airplanes. General Dynamics announced that it had spent $20 million to improve flight simulation capabilities for the F-16 and expected to spend a further $65 million over the next few years. Greece announced its decision to purchase forty F-16s.

December 1984 - NASA Langley Research Center revealed its development of a decoupler weapons carriage pylon, which demonstrated decoupling of vibrations which induced wing flutter on the F-16, beginning at Mach 0.7. The new pylon eliminated flutter up to Mach 0.95.

January 1985 - Singapore announced it would purchase F-16s. The U.S. Navy selected the F-16N as its adversary aircraft. An initial buy of fourteen, with twelve more projected later, was announced.

February 1985 - Delivery of the 998th F-16 was produced under the multinational coproduction program at Gosselies, Belgium.

April 1985 - Congress was notified of intent to supply Thailand with twelve F-16A/B aircraft.

May 1985 - First flight of the F-16AFTI equipped with FLIR and tracker system at Edwards AFB. The USAF announced it was negotiating fixed price contracts for upgraded performance versions of the Pratt & Whitney F-100 and the General Electric F-110 engines for the F-16.

June 1985 - General Dynamics submitted an unsolicited proposal to USAF for a 'cheap' version of the F-16C to counter interest in the Northrop F-20. The specially configured F-16 would be $2 million per copy cheaper than current production F-16s. Savings were accomplished by removal of some systems, although the basic aircraft retained the capability to perform air-to-air and air-to-ground missions, and could be upgraded with future enhancements to avionics or weapons carriage.

July 1985 - The second F-16 PACAF wing was activated at Misawa AB, Japan.

October 1985 - F-16 units took six of the top seven spots in Gunsmoke 85, the USAF worldwide fighter gunnery meet held at Nellis AFB, Nevada. The 419th TFW, AFRES, won first place, while the previous winner, the 50th TFW, took second.

December 1985 - Ramstein AB, Germany (USAFE) became the 28th worldwide base for F-16s and the first overseas base for F-16C/Ds.

January 1986 - F-16s pass the one million hour flight mark. The USAF announced that over 150 pilots had logged over 1,000 hours and that two pilots had over 2,000 hours in the F-16. The Thompson-CSF Atlis laser designator pod was qualified for use on F-16s for export to Pakistan. The F-16 was the first non-European aircraft to be qualified for the French pod.

February 1986 - The USAF increased its planned F-16 acquisition from 2,795 to 3,047.

March 1986 - The Republic of Korea Air Force took delivery of its first F-16 at Fort Worth. ROKAF was the first foreign air force to operate the F-16C/D. In remarks at the acceptance ceremony, LTGEN Suh Dong-Yull, Vice Chief of Staff of ROKAF, noted that ROKAF had gone from vintage T-6s in the 1950s to the latest state of the art fighter in the 1980s. General Dynamics announced production of upgrade kits for 770 F-16A/B aircraft of U.S., Belgian, Netherlands and Norwegian air forces.

July 1986 - The 1,000th USAF F-16 was delivered. It was the 1,572nd F-16 manufactured. The USAF began testing of the General Dynamics-built advanced tactical air reconnaissance system (ATARS), which would provide real-time tactical reconnaissance imagery through TV generated pictures. It was mounted on an F-16D for the initial testing. The USAF announced MSIP modifications that would assure growth of the F-16 into the 21st Century.

August 1986 - F-16 crews swept the top positions in TAC's Long Rifle 86 bombing competition. The USAF F-16 fleet exceeds 90% mission ready rate for the first month, far exceeding TAC standard. Indonesia signed a letter of agreement for twelve F-16A/B aircraft.

September 1986 - The first Air National Guard F-16 air defense unit was activated at Jacksonville, Florida. The 125th FIG began transition from the F-106A to the F-16A on 6 September. The second multi-year procurement agreement was signed for 720 F-16C/D aircraft to be manufactured in Fiscal Years 1986 - 1989.

October 1986 - The first F-16C arrived in Egypt after being delivered to the Egyptians at Fort Worth in August. The USAF announced the F-16A as the winner of the Air Defense competition for 270 strategic interceptor aircraft for use with ANG.

November 1986 - The USAF F-16A from the Air Force Flight Test Center, Edwards AFB, California launched a Royal Norwegian Air Force Penguin anti-ship missile at Point Mugu in tests of the operational capability upgrade.

December 1986 - The USAF F-16 fleet exceeded one million flight hours.

January 1987 - General Dynamics signed a formal agreement with the Hellenic Air Force for forty F-16C/D aircraft for Greece.

February 1987 - The first Israeli F-16C arrived in country.

March 1987 - Bahrain signed a letter of agreement to buy twelve F-16s. TAC Long Rifle II bombing competition was dominated by F-16 teams.

81-0777 was later transferred to the 612th Tactical Fighter Squadron, 401st Tactical Fighter Wing at Torrejon Air Base, Spain during March 1988. (Norm Taylor)

An F-16A (81-0763) of the 421st Tactical Fighter Squadron, 388th Tactical Fighter Wing at Offut Air Force Base on 21 August 1987. The tail codes are Black with White shadow shading. (George Cockle via David F. Brown)

April 1987 - 86th TFW, Ramstein AB, Germany converted to Block 30 F-16C/Ds and Misawa AB, Japan began conversion to F-16C/Ds while adding a second squadron. The first intercept of a Soviet aircraft in CONUS airspace made by an F-16 ADC version took place. The U.S. Navy introduced the first F-16N adversary aircraft at the Navy Fighter Weapons School - Top Gun, at NAS Miramar. The F-16N carried no gun or ground attack equipment, was powered by the F-110 GE 100 engine and was equipped with APG-66 radar.

May 1987 - The 50th TFW, Hahn AB, Germany won the USAF Daedalian and Phoenix Awards for best maintenance unit in the USAF and DOD, respectively. The F-16 Combined Test Force at Edwards AFB announced evaluation of the Advanced Tactical Air Reconnaissance System (ATARS). The CTF also completed evaluations of LANTIRN, and announced continuing work on Nuclear vibration flyaround, Larger engine inlet, AMRAAM, ADF configuration, APG-68 radar, GPS, HARM/Shrike integration, and foreign military sales aircraft configurations. Norway announced that it was considering replacement of its F-16s with Dassault-Breguet Rafale B or Saab-Scania JAS-39 Gripens.

June 1987 - The 19th TFS at Shaw AFB, SC set a new one-day squadron world record of 160 sorties in commemoration of the squadron's 70th anniversary. Great Falls, Montana became the second ANG F-16A/B air defense base. The first Block 32 F-16C/Ds were delivered to USAF for deployment to Luke AFB (AFRES) and Nellis AFB (57th FWW).

July 1987 - The Turkish Air Force received its first F-16 (F-16D 86-0191) at Fort Worth. Thailand announced plans to acquire an additional six F-16s. Testing of the two-pod LANTIRN system was completed at Eglin AFB, Florida. General Dynamics submitted an unsolicitied proposal to USAF for an upgraded version of the F-16 called "Agile Falcon." The enhanced version of the F-16 would be a relatively inexpensive alternative to acquisition of new aircraft for the NATO F-16 co-production partners. It included a larger wing, fuselage modifications, and extensive use of composites to offset weight increases. Spangdahlem AB, Germany activated F-16C/Ds in the Wild Weasel defense suppression role. F-16 teams swept USAFE's first Excalibur bombing competition, and dominated TAC's Long Rifle III competition.

September 1987 - The AFTI/F-16 program team received the Air Force Association's 1987 Theodore von Karman Award for most outstanding achievement in science and engineering. McConnell AFB activated the second ANG F-16 training site. The 432nd TFW, Misawa AB, Japan, won Sabre Spirit 87', the PACAF munitions competition. Eidetics International, Inc. unveiled aerodynamic modifications to existing F-16 fighters which they said would result in improved performance. The mods included shortening of fuselage strakes and modifying the nose radome.

October 1987 - Egypt signed a letter of agreement to purchase an additional forty F-16C/Ds with AIM-7 capability. Kunsan AB, Korea began conversion to F-16C/Ds. F-16 teams swept USAFE Excalibur II. The USAF Thunderbirds completed their first Pacific tour since 1959, performing in fourteen cities in ten countries. F-16 teams dominated Gunsmoke 87', USAF's worldwide bombing competition. The first Turkish F-16C/Ds arrived in country at Murted AB, while Luke AFB AFRES activated new Block 32 F-16C/Ds, becoming the first AFRES unit to get the latest version. NAS Key West activated its adversary F-16N unit, and Japan announced that it would develop a derivative version of the F-16 as its FS-X. General Dynamics displayed a Close Air Support (CAS) version of the F-16 featuring Maverick Missiles and a 30MM gun pod at a meeting in Washington, D.C. The USAF announced that it might develop "Agile Falcon" without allied participation if the European partners opted out of the program. The 3246th Test Wing at Eglin AFB, Florida conducted AGM-88 HARM and Shrike air-to-ground missile tests on the F-16. In routine static tests at Fort Worth, an F-16 wing buckled, causing USAF to put a temporary restriction on F-16 G loads.

November 1987 - The F-16 European co-production partners announced that they would evaluate the Agile Falcon upgrade to the F-16. The AFTI F-16 was brought out of retirement for new tests to evaluate advanced sensors in the CAS role. These sensors included a Collins advanced avionics suite, including ground-to-air data link.

December 1987 - Thailand signed a letter of agreement for six additional F-16s.

January 1988 - The Congress pressed NATO to pay for relocation of Spanish-based F-16s, which Spain was threatening to evict for political reasons.

February 1988 - Singapore accepted delivery of its first F-16, the 2,000th worldwide F-16. All eight of Singapore's F-16s would remain at Luke AFB, Arizona, where twelve pilots from the Singapore Air Force would receive training on the F-16. The conversion course was expected to take two years.

March 1988 - The USAF approved a pre-production development plan for "Agile Falcon." The re-configured AFTI F-16 returned to Edwards AFB for CAS tests.

April 1988 - F-16 teams dominated TAC's Long Rifle IV bombing competition at George AFB, California. German Defense Minister Manfred Woerner called for a halt to all F-16 flights over Germany following the second crash of an F-16 in Germany in a three week period. Two other crashes in the same period (A French Mirage F-1 and an Army OH-58) added to the minister's concern over low level military training flights.

May 1988 - Israel ordered more than sixty F-16C/D aircraft. Thailand took delivery of its first F-16A.

June 1988 - Denmark, the Netherlands and Norway signed a memorandum of understanding to take part in development and production of the "Agile Falcon." Korea ordered 4 F-16Ds. Congress was notified that Malaysia would buy six F-16As and two F-16Bs. A report released by the Pentagon blamed high interest rates and rampant inflation of the late 70s for a $33 billion cost overrun in the USAF F-16 program. USAFE took all of its aircraft out of service for two days for safety review following the crash of three F-16s on 29 June in Germany.

September 1988 - The worldwide F-16 fleet passed the two million hour milestone, with simultaneous flights by pilots from Belgium, Denmark, the Netherlands, Norway and USAFE.

October 1988 - The first launch of an AIM-7 Sparrow missile took place at the Pacific Missile Test Center, Point Mugu, California. The USAF began briefing Pentagon officials on the results of a study which concluded that a modified version of the F-16, called the A-16, would be the best replacement for the A-10.

November 1988 - Greece took delivery of its first F-16D at Fort Worth.

December 1988 - Air Force Systems Command endorsed moving ahead with an accelerated development schedule for the Combat Edge vest, which was projected to provide F-16 and F-15 pilots with greater protection against gravity-induced loss of consciousness (GLOC). "Agile Falcon" predevelopment was authorized. Pakistan signed an order for eleven additional F-16s. Block 50 development was authorized after the first Block 40 F-16 was delivered. The first Block 40 F-16 included provision for use of LANTIRN pods.

January 1989 - Greece received its first F-16s at Nea Anhialos Air Base. ROKAF ordered four additional F-16Ds. The first F-16s based in England were at RAF Bentwaters. The USAF Fiscal 1990-91 budget included plans to begin full-scale development of a new F-16 derivative aircraft, optimized for air superiority, but with CAS capability.

February 1989 - The first Aggressor F-16 was delivered in MiG-29 Fulcrum paint scheme. The first F-16 Air Defense Fighter retrofit

modification was completed. General Dynamics altered its marketing strategy to concentrate on upgrades to existing F-16s instead of the Agile Falcon, in response to world-wide tendencies towards defense economies. The Bush Administration announced that it was delaying F-16 technology transfer to Japan for their FS-X program, citing a report by Commerce Secretary Robert A. Mosbacher which delineated long-term concerns over the effect on the U.S. aerospace industry.

March 1989 - The number one F-16XL was returned to flight test status and returned to NASA for tests of sustained supersonic flight. The USAF announced that it was prepared to accept modest modifications to the F-16 and retain A-10s as an interim solution for close air support aircraft. Efforts to resolve the impasse on technology transfer to Japan for the FS-X aircraft failed, and negotiations were suspended.

May 1989 - The Bush Administration notified Congress that it had resolved questions of technology transfer to Japan for the FS-X and that the program was back on track. General Dynamics expected to receive about 75% of the $500 million U.S. share of the FS-X development work. The first F-16C Block 40 was deployed to Luke AFB. Full production of the Martin Marietta LANTIRN targeting pod was approved.

June 1989 - The first dedicated close air support (CAS) unit was activated at Syracuse, New York. Multi-year III long-lead funding was authorized for 600 USAF aircraft. An F-16 team won TAC's Long Rifle V bombing competition. The USAF announced that the 7th Air Force would convert to all F-16s, replacing F-4s and A-10s.

August 1989 - Eidetics International claimed that modifications it had proposed to the F-16 would allow the F-16 to perform "Pougachev's Cobra" maneuver, which had wowed them at the Paris Air Show in June when performed by a Soviet Su-27.

September 1989 - Pakistan signed for an additional sixty F-16A/Bs.

October 1989 - Indonesia took delivery of its first F-16A. An F-16 team won the USAFE Excalibur VI bombing competition.

November 1989 - General Electric proposed installation of the F110 GE 100 engine in newly built F-16A/Bs. The GE engine was 700 lbs heavier, as well as larger, than the Pratt & Whitney F100 engine installed in the F-16A/B, necessitating some structural changes for installation. Although the F110 engine was rated higher in thrust

An F-16C of the 57th Fighter Weapons Wing (FWW) on turn-out after takeoff from Nellis Air Force Base on 18 July 1991. The aircraft is carrying a Maverick air-to-surface missile on the outboard wing pylon. (Ted Carlson)

An F-16A (81-0763) of the 421st Tactical Fighter Squadron, 388th Tactical Fighter Wing at Offut Air Force Base on 21 August 1987. The tail codes are Black with White shadow shading. (George Cockle via David F. Brown)

April 1987 - 86th TFW, Ramstein AB, Germany converted to Block 30 F-16C/Ds and Misawa AB, Japan began conversion to F-16C/Ds while adding a second squadron. The first intercept of a Soviet aircraft in CONUS airspace made by an F-16 ADC version took place. The U.S. Navy introduced the first F-16N adversary aircraft at the Navy Fighter Weapons School - Top Gun, at NAS Miramar. The F-16N carried no gun or ground attack equipment, was powered by the F-110 GE 100 engine and was equipped with APG-66 radar.

May 1987 - The 50th TFW, Hahn AB, Germany won the USAF Daedalian and Phoenix Awards for best maintenance unit in the USAF and DOD, respectively. The F-16 Combined Test Force at Edwards AFB announced evaluation of the Advanced Tactical Air Reconnaissance System (ATARS). The CTF also completed evaluations of LANTIRN, and announced continuing work on Nuclear vibration flyaround, Larger engine inlet, AMRAAM, ADF configuration, APG-68 radar, GPS, HARM/Shrike integration, and foreign military sales aircraft configurations. Norway announced that it was considering replacement of its F-16s with Dassault-Breguet Rafale B or Saab-Scania JAS-39 Gripens.

June 1987 - The 19th TFS at Shaw AFB, SC set a new one-day squadron world record of 160 sorties in commemoration of the squadron's 70th anniversary. Great Falls, Montana became the second ANG F-16C/Ds air defense base. The first Block 32 F-16C/Ds were delivered to USAF for deployment to Luke AFB (AFRES) and Nellis AFB (57th FWW).

July 1987 - The Turkish Air Force received its first F-16 (F-16D 86-0191) at Fort Worth. Thailand announced plans to acquire an additional six F-16s. Testing of the two-pod LANTIRN system was completed at Eglin AFB, Florida. General Dynamics submitted an unsolicited proposal to USAF for an upgraded version of the F-16 called "Agile Falcon." The enhanced version of the F-16 would be a relatively inexpensive alternative to acquisition of new aircraft for the NATO F-16 co-production partners. It included a larger wing, fuselage modifications, and extensive use of composites to offset weight increases. Spangdahlem AB, Germany activated F-16C/Ds in the Wild Weasel defense suppression role. F-16 teams swept USAFE's first Excalibur bombing competition, and dominated TAC's Long Rifle III competition.

September 1987 - The AFTI/F-16 program team received the Air Force Association's 1987 Theodore von Karman Award for most outstanding achievement in science and engineering. McConnell AFB activated the second ANG F-16 training site. The 432nd TFW, Misawa AB, Japan, won Sabre Spirit 87', the PACAF munitions competition. Eidetics International, Inc. unveiled aerodynamic modifications to existing F-16 fighters which they said would result in improved performance. The mods included shortening of fuselage strakes and modifying the nose radome.

October 1987 - Egypt signed a letter of agreement to purchase an additional forty F-16C/Ds with AIM-7 capability. Kunsan AB, Korea began conversion to F-16C/Ds. F-16 teams swept USAFE Excalibur II. The USAF Thunderbirds completed their first Pacific tour since 1959, performing in fourteen cities in ten countries. F-16 teams dominated Gunsmoke 87', USAF's worldwide bombing competition. The first Turkish F-16C/Ds arrived in country at Murted AB, while Luke AFB AFRES activated new Block 32 F-16C/Ds, becoming the first AFRES unit to get the latest version. NAS Key West activated its adversary F-16N unit, and Japan announced that it would develop a derivative version of the F-16 as its FS-X. General Dynamics displayed a Close Air Support (CAS) version of the F-16 featuring Maverick Missiles and a 30MM gun pod at a meeting in Washington, D.C. The USAF announced that it might develop "Agile Falcon" without allied participation if the European partners opted out of the program. The 3246th Test Wing at Eglin AFB, Florida conducted AGM-88 HARM and Shrike air-to-ground missile tests on the F-16. In routine static tests at Fort Worth, an F-16 wing buckled, causing USAF to put a temporary restriction on F-16 G loads.

November 1987 - The F-16 European co-production partners announced that they would evaluate the Agile Falcon upgrade to the F-16. The AFTI F-16 was brought out of retirement for new tests to evaluate advanced sensors in the CAS role. These sensors included a Collins advanced avionics suite, including ground-to-air data link.

December 1987 - Thailand signed a letter of agreement for six additional F-16s.

January 1988 - The Congress pressed NATO to pay for relocation of Spanish-based F-16s, which Spain was threatening to evict for political reasons.

February 1988 - Singapore accepted delivery of its first F-16, the 2,000th worldwide F-16. All eight of Singapore's F-16s would remain at Luke AFB, Arizona, where twelve pilots from the Singapore Air Force would receive training on the F-16. The conversion course was expected to take two years.

March 1988 - The USAF approved a pre-production development plan for "Agile Falcon." The re-configured AFTI F-16 returned to Edwards AFB for CAS tests.

April 1988 - F-16 teams dominated TAC's Long Rifle IV bombing competition at George AFB, California. German Defense Minister Manfred Woerner called for a halt to all F-16 flights over Germany following the second crash of an F-16 in Germany in a three week period. Two other crashes in the same period (A French Mirage F-1 and an Army OH-58) added to the minister's concern over low level military training flights.

May 1988 - Israel ordered more than sixty F-16C/D aircraft. Thailand took delivery of its first F-16A.

June 1988 - Denmark, the Netherlands and Norway signed a memorandum of understanding to take part in development and production of the "Agile Falcon." Korea ordered 4 F-16Ds. Congress was notified that Malaysia would buy six F-16As and two F-16Bs. A report released by the Pentagon blamed high interest rates and rampant inflation of the late 70s for a $33 billion cost overrun in the USAF F-16 program. USAFE took all of its aircraft out of service for two days for safety review following the crash of three F-16s on 29 June in Germany.

September 1988 - The worldwide F-16 fleet passed the two million hour milestone, with simultaneous flights by pilots from Belgium, Denmark, the Netherlands, Norway and USAFE.

October 1988 - The first launch of an AIM-7 Sparrow missile took place at the Pacific Missile Test Center, Point Mugu, California. The USAF began briefing Pentagon officials on the results of a study which concluded that a modified version of the F-16, called the A-16, would be the best replacement for the A-10.

November 1988 - Greece took delivery of its first F-16D at Fort Worth.

December 1988 - Air Force Systems Command endorsed moving ahead with an accelerated development schedule for the Combat Edge vest, which was projected to provide F-16 and F-15 pilots with greater protection against gravity-induced loss of consciousness (GLOC). "Agile Falcon" predevelopment was authorized. Pakistan signed an order for eleven additional F-16s. Block 50 development was authorized after the first Block 40 F-16 was delivered. The first Block 40 F-16 included provision for use of LANTIRN pods.

January 1989 - Greece received its first F-16s at Nea Anhialos Air Base. ROKAF ordered four additional F-16Ds. The first F-16s based in England were at RAF Bentwaters. The USAF Fiscal 1990-91 budget included plans to begin full-scale development of a new F-16 derivative aircraft, optimized for air superiority, but with CAS capability.

February 1989 - The first Aggressor F-16 was delivered in MiG-29 Fulcrum paint scheme. The first F-16 Air Defense Fighter retrofit modification was completed. General Dynamics altered its marketing strategy to concentrate on upgrades to existing F-16s instead of the Agile Falcon, in response to world-wide tendencies towards defense economies. The Bush Administration announced that it was delaying F-16 technology transfer to Japan for their FS-X program, citing a report by Commerce Secretary Robert A. Mosbacher which delineated long-term concerns over the effect on the U.S. aerospace industry.

March 1989 - The number one F-16XL was returned to flight test status and returned to NASA for tests of sustained supersonic flight. The USAF announced that it was prepared to accept modest modifications to the F-16 and retain A-10s as an interim solution for close air support aircraft. Efforts to resolve the impasse on technology transfer to Japan for the FS-X aircraft failed, and negotiations were suspended.

May 1989 - The Bush Administration notified Congress that it had resolved questions of technology transfer to Japan for the FS-X and that the program was back on track. General Dynamics expected to receive about 75% of the $500 million U.S. share of the FS-X development work. The first F-16C Block 40 was deployed to Luke AFB. Full production of the Martin Marietta LANTIRN targeting pod was approved.

June 1989 - The first dedicated close air support (CAS) unit was activated at Syracuse, New York. Multi-year III long-lead funding was authorized for 600 USAF aircraft. An F-16 team won TAC's Long Rifle V bombing competition. The USAF announced that the 7th Air Force would convert to all F-16s, replacing F-4s and A-10s.

August 1989 - Eidetics International claimed that modifications it had proposed to the F-16 would allow the F-16 to perform "Pougachev's Cobra" maneuver, which had wowed them at the Paris Air Show in June when performed by a Soviet Su-27.

September 1989 - Pakistan signed for an additional sixty F-16A/Bs.

October 1989 - Indonesia took delivery of its first F-16A. An F-16 team won the USAFE Excalibur VI bombing competition.

November 1989 - General Electric proposed installation of the F110 GE 100 engine in newly built F-16A/Bs. The GE engine was 700 lbs heavier, as well as larger, than the Pratt & Whitney F100 engine installed in the F-16A/B, necessitating some structural changes for installation. Although the F110 engine was rated higher in thrust

An F-16C of the 57th Fighter Weapons Wing (FWW) on turn-out after takeoff from Nellis Air Force Base on 18 July 1991. The aircraft is carrying a Maverick air-to-surface missile on the outboard wing pylon. (Ted Carlson)

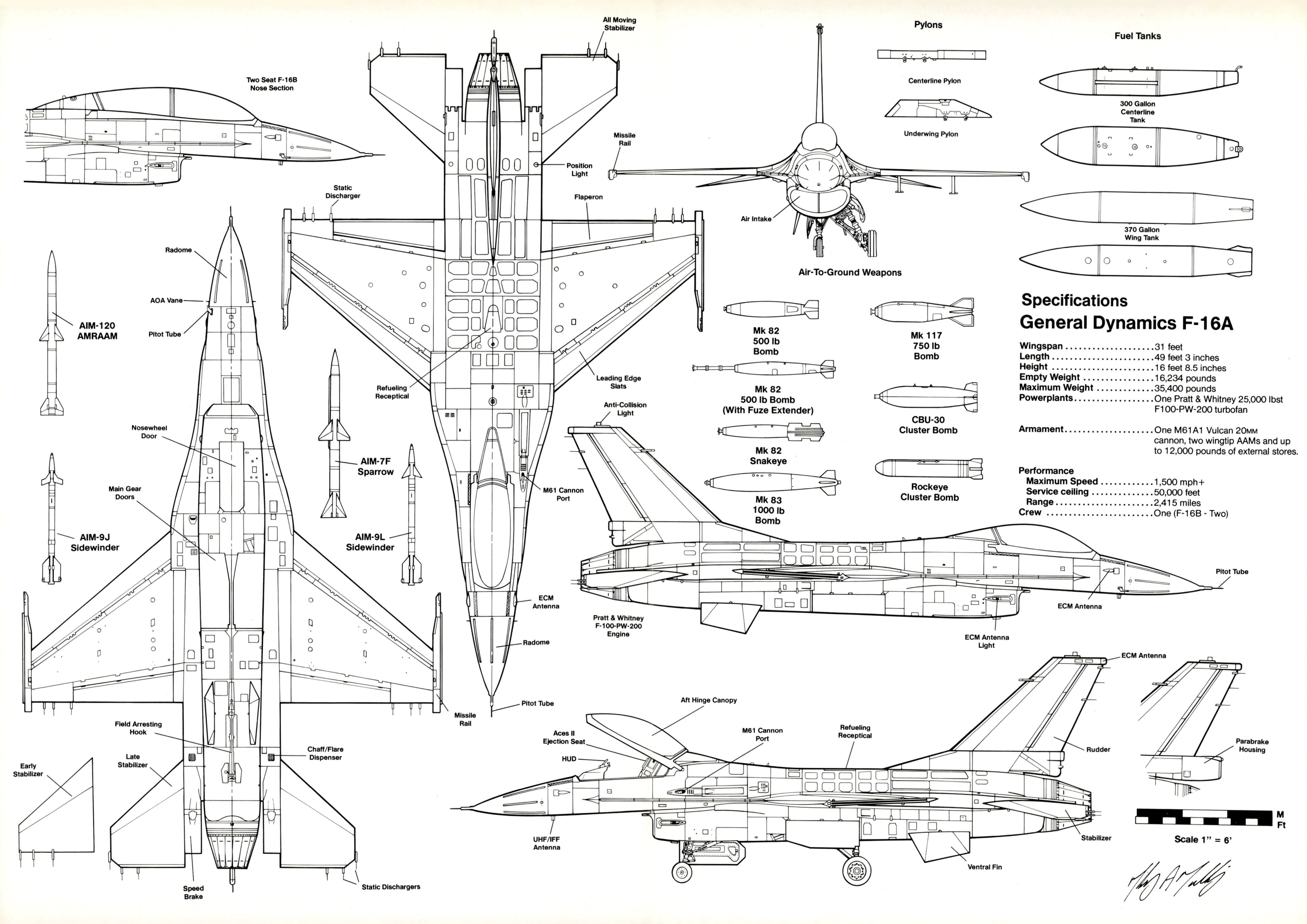

Two Seat F-16B Nose Section
All Moving Stabilizer
Pylons
Centerline Pylon
Underwing Pylon
Fuel Tanks
300 Gallon Centerline Tank
370 Gallon Wing Tank
Missile Rail
Position Light
Flaperon
Static Discharger
Air Intake
Air-To-Ground Weapons
Radome
AOA Vane
Pitot Tube
AIM-120 AMRAAM
AIM-7F Sparrow
AIM-9L Sidewinder
AIM-9J Sidewinder
Main Gear Doors
Nosewheel Door
Refueling Receptical
Anti-Collision Light
Leading Edge Slats
Mk 82 500 lb Bomb
Mk 117 750 lb Bomb
Mk 82 500 lb Bomb (With Fuze Extender)
Mk 82 Snakeye
CBU-30 Cluster Bomb
Mk 83 1000 lb Bomb
Rockeye Cluster Bomb
M61 Cannon Port
ECM Antenna
Radome
Pratt & Whitney F-100-PW-200 Engine
Pitot Tube
ECM Antenna
ECM Antenna Light
Missile Rail
Pitot Tube
Early Stabilizer
Late Stabilizer
Field Arresting Hook
Chaff/Flare Dispenser
Speed Brake
Static Dischargers
Aces II Ejection Seat
HUD
UHF/IFF Antenna
Aft Hinge Canopy
M61 Cannon Port
Refueling Receptical
ECM Antenna
Rudder
Parabrake Housing
Stabilizer
Ventral Fin
Specifications
General Dynamics F-16A
Wingspan ....31 feet
Length ....49 feet 3 inches
Height ....16 feet 8.5 inches
Empty Weight ....16,234 pounds
Maximum Weight ....35,400 pounds
Powerplants................One Pratt & Whitney 25,000 lbst F100-PW-200 turbofan
Armament...................One M61A1 Vulcan 20MM cannon, two wingtip AAMs and up to 12,000 pounds of external stores.
Performance
Maximum Speed ....1,500 mph+
Service ceiling ....50,000 feet
Range ....2,415 miles
Crew ....One (F-16B - Two)
M
Ft
Scale 1" = 6'

A 57th Fighter Weapons Wing F-16C armed with a load of four Cluster Bomb Units (CBUs) climbs out enroute to one of the the Nellis bombing ranges on 24 July 1990. (Ted Carlson)

than the F-100 engine, a larger inlet was required to achieve its full potential. An Air Force F-16C was successfully tested with the larger engine inlet.

December 1989 - The first Indonesian F-16s arrived in-country. The 2,500th worldwide F-16 was delivered.

January 1990 - Singapore's first F-16 arrived in-country. General Dynamics and associate contractors received incentive awards for exceeding F-16C reliability goals.

March 1990 - Bahrain received its first F-16C/D aircraft.

April 1990 - General Dynamics planners stated that they believed they could keep derivatives of the F-16 fighter in production through 2005 or beyond by careful addition of aerodynamic and engine enhancements. Some of the modifications could come about if USAF cut back on its active force, making older F-16A/Bs available to friendly nations. One F-16 derivative, known as the F-16AT or Falcon 21, was gaining stature as an alternative to the ATF contenders. The Falcon 21 would use the F-16XL design, along with one of the proposed ATF engines.

May 1990 - Bahrain received their first F-16C/D.

June 1990 - Congress was notified that Portugal intended to purchase twenty F-16A/Bs. Egypt signed a letter of agreement for six F-16s in addition to the forty already purchased in its third F-16 buy. USAF sources indicated that they intended to push for replacement of their RF-4C reconnaissance aircraft with ATARS-equipped F-16s. The announced plan would equip 150 existing block 30 F-16s with the advanced tactical air reconnaissance system, redesignating them RF-16s. The possibility of equipping RF-16s with terrain following radar, helmet-mounted display and head-steered forward-looking infrared systems was also advanced. Pentagon planners said they were fearful that USAF's decision to postpone beyond Fiscal 1997 whether or not to upgrade the F-16 airframe or develop a new multi-role fighter would leave the service with a large number of less-capable F-16s. Meanwhile, it was announced that operational F-16s would be retrofitted with automatic target handover system (ATHS), a digital data link which allowed for transmission of ground target information. Future F-16s were to be equipped with the Improved Data Modem (IDM), beginning in 1993. IDM was developed by the Naval Research Laboratory. General Dynamics revealed preliminary plans for the Falcon 21 which showed a trapezoidal delta wing, rather than the F-16XL cranked-arrow design. GD also proposed the F-16 "Agile Falcon" to Israel as a replacement for their current fleet of F-16s.

July 1990 - The USAF announced that it was examining methods for increasing the F-16's weapons-carrying capabilities. These included installation of six independently-targeted weapons into a single streamlined pod. The weapons were designated Low-Cost Advanced Technology Missiles (LOCATM) and the carrier was an Expend-able Intelligent Multiple Ejector Rack (XIMER). The Air Force Development Test Center at Eglin AFB, Florida said these new designs would decrease drag, significantly extending the F-16s range and speed. The six "smart" missiles were to be equipped with "fire and forget" seeker heads.

September 1990 - The USAF announced that it was developing a VISTA (variable stability in-flight simulator test aircraft) F-16 to replace the NT-33A operated since 1957 under contract by Calspan Corp. The VISTA F-16 would be modeled on the Israeli modification of the F-16D, equipped with heavier landing gear and a dorsal fin to accommodate additional avionics.

October 1990 - Dassault Electronique announced that it would produce a new electronic warfare system for Belgian F-16s. The Carapace EWS-16 could measure the bearing to threat radars to within 1 degree. Carapace's interferometer antenna array would be belly mounted under the F-16 air intake.

December 1990 - Portugal became the 17th nation to order F-16s. The USAF dropped its plan to develop an A-16 close air support aircraft, announcing that it would instead retrofit up to 400 existing Block 30 F-16C/Ds with new equipment to perform the mission.

January 1991 - Operation DESERT STORM begins with co-ordinated attacks against Iraq on 17 January. F-16s would perform 25% of all sorties (300-400 daily), adding up to 13,500 by war's end. Mission capable rate for F-16s was 95.2%.

March 1991 - Congress was notified that Egypt would purchase forty-six F-16s in its fourth order. The government of Korea announced that it had selected the F-16 for its Korean Fighter Program, which would consist of 120 aircraft. This reversed the decision, made 15 months previously, to buy F/A-18s. The decision was driven by budgetary limitations. The change would save the Korean government more than $1 billion over the following ten years.

April 1991 - Egypt signed its fourth F-16 purchase, following congressional approval of the sale.

May 1991 - Belgium, Denmark, the Netherlands and Norway reaffirmed their commitment to the USAF/General Dynamics F-16A/B Mid-Life Update (MLU) program by completing letters of acceptance. The MLU would provide advanced avionics for earlier generation F-16s. The upgrade also included extensive cockpit enhancements including multi-function displays modeled on the F-16C/D cockpit. Over 530 aircraft would be included in the program which was expected to last for five years, with the first upgrade kits delivered in the mid-90s. The Navy grounded its fleet of twenty-six F-16N fighters due to structural cracking in the center fuselage area. USAF F-16s had experienced similar cracking, but a difference in philosophy kept the Air Force flying, while the Navy grounded their airplanes until the cracks could be repaired.

June 1991 - F-16s of the Florida Air National Guard fired live AIM-7 missiles for the first time in successful tests at Tyndall AFB, Florida. The first ANG unit flying the ADF version of the F-16, the 114th TFTS, Kingsley Field, Oregon announced that it was flying about 30% more missions than it did with the F-4 Phantom. The 114th transitioned to the F-16 in mid-1989. The first F-16C produced

An F-16D of the 57th FWW leaves Nellis AFB loaded with Maverick air-to-ground anti-tank missiles on 18 July 1991 during one of the *Desert Flag* training missions. (Ted Carlson)

in Israel's third order was delivered at Fort Worth. The first interception of a Soviet Blackjack bomber was recorded by Norwegian Air Force F-16's from 331 squadron, based at Bodo, Norway.

July 1991 - General Dynamics received the first major subcontracts for FS-X development work to be performed in the United States for Mitsubishi Heavy Industries of Japan. Congress was notified of Turkey's request to order eighty additional F-16C/Ds, and of Morocco's request to purchase twenty refurbished F-16A/B aircraft from U.S. inventory. The USAF announced that it would modify or scrap all existing F-16s due to structural cracks. All pre-Block 50 aircraft would require some modification. Block 10 and 15 aircraft would be too expensive to repair, while repair of later versions was estimated to cost up to $280 million.

September 1991 - Congress was notified of Thailand's request for eighteen additional F-16A/B aircraft. General Dynamics, General Electric and the Israeli Air Force agreed to participate in a joint program to demonstrate vectored thrust in the F-16. The Israelis were contacted after USAF declined to participate in the the flight test program.

Pratt & Whitney revealed plans to upgrade the F-100 engine from 29,000 lbst to 35,000 lbst by the mid-1990s.

October 1991 - The Korean and U.S. governments signed an agreement for the Foreign Military Sales portion of the 120 aircraft Korean Fighter Program. General Dynamics and Samsung signed contracts for the commercial and licensed production portions. The USAF accepted the first Block 50 F-16C at Fort Worth.

November 1991 - Morocco and the U.S. Government signed an agreement for Morocco's purchase of twenty F-16A/Bs to be taken from USAF inventory. Morocco thus became the 18th country to fly the F-16. USAF CAPT Goose Gosselin became the 1,000th pilot to log 1,000 hours in the F-16.

December 1991 - The number of F-16s delivered worldwide was 3,000 with 753 more under contract and negotiations for another 100 underway. Thai and U.S. governments signed an agreement formalizing Thailand's follow-on purchase of eighteen F-16A/Bs for 1994 delivery.

This F-16C (86-0220) carries an aggressor camouflage scheme of Light Gray and Blue Gray uppersurfaces over Light Gray undersurfaces. This scheme represents the type of camouflage schemes seen on MiG-29s. The checkerboard band on the tail is Black and Yellow. (Ted Carlson)

The night capabilities of the LANTIRN-equipped F-16D are demonstrated in this simulated cockpit display on the CRT and HUD. The F-16C was the first Viper variant to carry the LANTIRN system. (General Dynamics)

An F-16C of the 57th FWW on the flight line at Nellis AFB during January of 1992. The aircraft carries a falcon head insignia in Dark Gray on the vertical fin. (Author)

This F-16C (86-0220) parked on the ramp at Nellis AFB on 10 June 1988 carries the markings of the commander, Tactical Fighter Weapons Center. This unit is tasked with developing USAF fighter tactics for a variety of USAF fighters including the F-16. (Brian Rogers via David F. Brown)

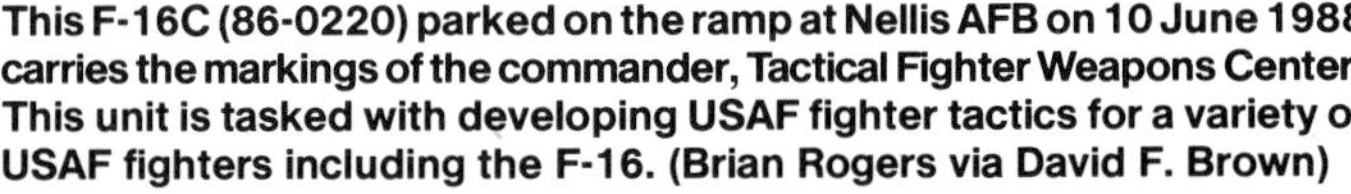

An F-16B-10-CF (79-0430) of the 430th TFS, 474th TFW, based at Nellis AFB, on the ramp at Shaw AFB for a stop-over while enroute to Italy on 30 October 1986. The 474th TFW was inactivated on 1 October 1989. (Norm Taylor)

The number seven F-16A of the USAF Thunderbirds was flown by the the unit's Logistics Officer, MAJ Dave Janik. The aircraft was taking up position for refueling by an ANG KC-135 while the team was enroute to an East Coast air show from their home base at Nellis. (Author)

The number eight Thunderbird is a two-seat F-16B that is normally assigned to the team narrator. The F-16B is used to give media rides to the press/TV people and other VIPs at the many show sites visited by the team. (David F. Brown)

An F-16D-30-CF (87-0380) of the 14th TFS, 432nd TFW, based at Misawa Air Base, Japan is parked in a revetment at Kunsan Air Base, Korea on 20 June 1991 during a unit deployment to Korea. (Paul Hunt via Norm Taylor)

An F-16C-25-CF (84-1385) of the 10th TFS, 50th TFW based at Hahn AB, Germany takes off from Shaw AFB, SC on 5 June 1987. The 50th TFW was the first European F-16 unit to receive the LANTIRN-capable Block 40 F-16C and deployed them to Saudi Arabia for Operation DESERT STORM. Ironically, they were one of the units scheduled for deactivation in a draw-down of U.S. forces in Europe following the dissolution of the Soviet Union in 1990-1991. (Norman E. Taylor)

An F-16C of the 10th TFS, 50th TFW takes on fuel from a KC-135R, while the rest of the flight waits their turn. The 50th TFW was based at Hahn AB, Germany and transitioned to the F-16 from F-4 Phantoms during 1982. The aircraft in the foreground carries Black/Yellow/Red bands on the intake and tail, identifying it as the Wing Commander's aircraft. (General Dynamics via David F. Brown)

This F-16C of the 313th TFS, 50th TFW is parked on the ramp at Nellis AFB, Nevada for a Red Flag exercise during July of 1989. It carries two 370 gallon external fuel tanks, six 500 lb low drag bombs, AIM-9 AAMs and an ALQ-131 ECM pod. (Ted Carlson)

This F-16C of the 10th TFS, 50th TFW carries a "special shape" (nuclear weapon aerodynamic training round) on station 8, attached to the AIM-9 Sidewinder missile launch rail. (General Dynamics)

This F-16A of the Multinational Test and Evaluation unit, attached to the 388th Tactical Fighter Wing, Hill AFB, Utah is armed with an AIM-9 Sidewinder on station 8 and an SUU practice bomb dispenser on station 7. (Roy Chismar)

An F-16A-15-CF (83-1079) of the 613th TFS, 401st TFW based at Torrejon AB, Spain is parked on the ramp at Shaw AFB, SC on 5 March 1987 during a visit. The open access panel on the fuselage is for the external power receptacle. (Norman E. Taylor)

This F-16A-15-CF (82-0954) of the 613th TFS, 401st TFW at Torrejon AB, Spain, is configured for a long deployment with three external fuel tanks and a travel pod on the outboard wing station. (Norman E. Taylor)

Homestead AFB, Florida is the home base for this F-16B of the 309th TFS, Wild Ducks, one of the squadrons assigned to the 31st Tactical Fighter Wing. The tail band is Dark Blue with a thin White outline and the name is in White letters. (David F. Brown)

This F-16C of the 19th TFS, Gamecocks, 363rd TFW, home based at Shaw AFB, S.C. was at Nellis AFB for Desert Flag training on 5 July 1991. The aircraft was configured with AMRAAM missiles on stations 1 and 9, a Sidewinder training round on the outboard wing pylon, bombs on the center pylon, fuel tanks on the inboard pylons and an ECM pod on the centerline. (Ted Carlson)

This F-16C of the 308th TFS, Knights, 31st TFW is configured with Triple Ejector Racks (TERs) on the outboard wind stations. The aircraft was flying out of Nellis AFB for a Desert Flag mission on 18 July 1991. (Ted Carlson)

An F-16A of the 17th Tactical Fighter Squadron, 363rd Tactical Fighter Wing chocked on the ramp at Shaw AFB, SC during April of 1985. The squadron carried the unit nickname, Owls, in Black on the White fin band. (David F. Brown)

An F-16C of the 17th TFS, 363rd TFW at Selfridge AFB, Michigan on 5 August 1990. The aircraft was hooked into a starter/power unit in preparation for its participation in an open house air show. Within a week the *Hooters* would be on their way to the Persian Gulf. (Author)

A very clean F-16C 84-0233 of the 33rd TFS, Falcons, 363rd TFW prepares to taxi for a 15 September 1986 mission from Shaw AFB. The 363rd TFW was the first operational unit to get the F-16C/D. (George Cockle via David F. Brown)

A new production F-16C (84-0217) of the 17th TFS, 363rd TFW on the ramp at Shaw AFB on 17 September 1986. The name, Hooters, was in Black on a White tail band. The squadron insignia was carried on the air intake cover. (George Cockle via David F. Brown)

The A-16 was proposed as a replacement for the A-10 in the Close Air Support (CAS) role. This A-16C-25-CF (83-1144) of the 33rd TFS, 363rd TFW was painted in the European One Lizard camouflage scheme and was the only aircraft so designated and painted in the wing. When the A-16 idea was dropped, the aircraft was repainted in standard F-16 colors. (Norm Taylor)

This F-16A of No 350 Squadron, Belgium Air Force is carrying a special paint scheme for the squadron's 50th anniversary. The BAF was one of the four original NATO air forces to receive the F-16.

This F-16D of the Israeli Defense Force/Air Force (IAF/AF *Heyl Ha'Avir*) has a modified dorsal spine that is used to carry Israeli-built avionics for SAM suppression (Wild Weasel) missions.

An F-16C-25-CF (84-1219) of the 19th TFS, 363rd TFW on the ramp at Shaw AFB, SC on 19 May 1986. The aircraft carries a Red-headed rooster with a Yellow beak on the dorsal fin and the squadron nickname, Gamecocks, on the tail band. It is armed with a single AGM-65 Maverick missile. (Norm Taylor)

On 15 November 1991, USAF Captain 'Goose' Gosselin, an instructor with the 58th Tactical Training Wing, became the 1,000th pilot to log 1,000 flight hours in the F-16. (General Dynamics)

An operational family portrait of the F-16 family with (front to rear) F-16D,C,B and A variants of the 58th Tactical Training Wing on the taxiway of Luke AFB, Arizona. The F-16C/D versions are from the 312th TFTS Scorpions, the B model is from the 311th Sidewinders and the A model is from the 310th Tophats. The 58th TTW provides F-16 conversion training for USAF and some foreign F-16 operators. (General Dynamics)

An F-16C-30-CF 85-1412 of the 512th TFS, 86th TFW, Ramstein AB, Germany at Shaw AFB on 16 October 1987. The 86th was the first overseas unit to operate the F-16C, taking delivery of their first aircraft on 21 December 1985. They were also the first to get the Block 30 F-16C, powered by the General Electric F110-GE-100 turbofan engine. (Norm Taylor)

A sharkmouthed F-16D of the 480th TFS, 52nd TFW based at Spang-dahlem AB, Germany. The 52nd Wing operated both F-16C/D and F-4G aircraft in three squadrons as "Hunter-Killer" teams in the Wild Weasel mission. (General Dynamics)

A four aircraft team of F-16As of the 347th Tactical Fighter Wing based at Moody AFB, Georgia on the line at Nellis AFB for the "Gunsmoke 89" gunnery competition. (David F. Brown)

An F-16C and F-4G of the 480th TFS, 52nd TFW in formation over Germany. Both are armed with the SAM hunters principle weapon, the AGM-88A HARM anti-radiation missile and both are marked with the unit's distinctive black sharkmouth. (General Dynamics via Dave Brown)

An F-16A of the 347th during judging for the weapons loading competition at "Gunsmoke 89." The aircraft carries an ACMI pod on station one and a Red/Silver/Blue-White checkerboard band on the tail, representing the three squadrons of the wing (68th, 69th, 70th TFS). (David F. Brown)

This F-16A of No 349 Squadron, Belgium Air Force carries the special paint scheme applied for the squadron's 45th anniversary.

An F-16C of the 526th Tactical Fighter Squadron, 86th Tactical Fighter Wing flown by BGEN Cecil W. Powell, commander of the 316th Air Division during 1986.

This Red tailed F-16A was flown by No 322 Squadron, Royal Netherlands Air Force. The tail markings were applied to celebrate the squadron's 40th anniversary.

FA-62 was an F-16A specially painted for the Belgian Air Force Tiger Meet team.

These special markings were applied to this F-16A of No 312 Squadron of the Royal Netherlands Air Force to celebrate the 75th anniversary of the *Koninklijke Luchtmacht*. The squadron was based at Volkel Air Base.

This F-16B carries the Black and Red sharkmouth marking of the 52nd Tactical Fighter Wing at Spangdahlem Air Base, Germany.

F-16C of the 512th TFS, 86th TFW Ramstein AB, Germany.

The AFTI F-16A was flown under a joint USAF/NASA program. The aircraft carries the emblem of the Aeronautical Systems Division on the fin.

Markings carried by No 31 Squadron, Belgian AF for the Fairford Tiger Meet 1991.

Markings carried by No 313 Squadron, RNethAF for the Fairford Tiger Meet 1991.

An F-16A of the 526th Tactical Fighter Squadron, 86th Tactical Fighter Wing on the ramp outside of its blastproof shelter at Ramstein Air Base, Germany.

An F-16C-30-CF (86-0308) of the 8th TFW on the apron of Kunsan AB, Korea during April of 1991. Kunsan was the first overseas F-16 base. The 8th TFW Wolfpack is comprised of the 35th and 80th Tactical Fighter Squadrons. (Paul Hunt via Norm Taylor)

This F-16C of the 432nd Tactical Fighter Wing shares the ramp with other F-16 units during "Gunsmoke 89." The aircraft carried special tail codes (432TFW) for the competition. (David F. Brown)

Another F-16C of the 432nd TFW 1989 "Gunsmoke" team returns to Nellis after an 11 October 1989 mission. The aircraft is armed with a Blue painted dummy Mk 82 low drag bomb on the outboard wing station. (Ted Carlson)

An F-16A-5-CF (79-0320) of the 157th TFS Swamp Foxes, South Carolina Air National Guard during September of 1984. The 157th was the first Air Guard unit to receive the F-16, converting from the A-7D Corsair II during 1983. (Don Linn via Norm Taylor)

A flight of four South Carolina Air National Guard F-16As formate on a KC-135E Stratotanker of the Tennessee ANG during a practice mission flown in September of 1984. (Don Linn via Norm Taylor)

An F-16A-10-CF (79-0333) of the 127th TFS, Michigan Air National Guard chocked on the ramp at Travis Field, Savannah, Georgia on 11 April 1991. (Norm Taylor)

(Above) The *Batmobile* carried ten DESERT STORM combat mission markings on the nose. The F-16 was assigned to the 17th TFS, 363rd TFW. (Norm Taylor)

(Below) *Sweet but deadly* was the name carried by this F-16C (83-0158) of the 33rd TFS Falcons during DESERT STORM. Warren Trask was a very accomplished 363rd TFW artist whose nose art enlivened their F-16s. (Norm Taylor)

Warren Trask's Desert Shield marking for the 363rd TFW was done in shades of Gray except for the Orange sky and Blue sea behind the Falcon. It was carried throughout DESERT SHIELD and DESERT STORM. (Norm Taylor)

Thirty-seven combat mission markings were carried above the 'RESCUE' arrow on this F-16 flown by MAJ Roger "Ramjet" Yauchzy. (Norm Taylor)

(Above) An F-16A of the 188th Tactical Fighter Group, Arkansas Air National Guard based out of Fort Smith Municipal Airport. The Flying Razorbacks converted to the F-16A from the F-4C Phantom II during June of 1988. (General Dynamics)

(Below) This F-16A of the 159th FIS, Florida ANG based at Jacksonville, Florida is an F-16A Air Defense Force variant. The ADF version has several external identifying features including the horizontal bulges on the base of the vertical tail caused by installation of a Bendix/King AN/ARC-200 high frequency radio. (Norm Taylor)

(Above) Another identification feature of the F-16A ADF variant are the blade antennas carried just forward of the canopy. These are part of Teledyne/E Systems MK XII Advanced IFF system. (Norm Taylor)

(Below) An F-16A-15-CF (81-0675) of the 159th FIS, 125th TFG, Florida ANG at Jacksonville on 11 April 1991. The F-16 won the competition for a replacement for F-106 and F-4 Air Defense Interceptors largely because it was available in large enough numbers and could be modified to carry the necessary armament. (Norm Taylor)

This F-16A is assigned to the 134th FIS. The Green Mountain Boys of the 158th TFG, Vermont ANG take their name from the famous unit led by Revolutionary War hero Ethan Allen. The 134th FIS converted from the F-4 in June 1986. (David F. Brown)

This F-16A (79-0354) of the 906th TFG (AFRES) is home based at Wright Patterson AFB, Ohio. The aircraft is armed with 2,000 pound bombs and carries an ALQ-119 ECM pod on the centerline for a training mission at Nellis AFB during a Desert Flag exercise on 8 May 1991. (Ted Carlson)

An F-16A of the 121st TFS, 113th TFW, Washington D.C. Air National Guard. The D.C. Guard received its first F-16s during January of 1990 as replacement for F-4 Phantoms. They are based at Andrews AFB, Maryland.

This F-16A ADF belongs to the 114th TFTS, Oregon ANG based out of Kingsley Field, Klamath Falls. The unit is the training unit for ANG air defense pilots and transitioned from Phantoms during 1989. 81-0811 was landing at MCAS El Toro, California on 4 May 1990. (Ted Carlson)

An F-16A ADF of the 178th FIS, 119th FIG, North Dakota ANG. The "Happy Hooligans" have a long history of performing the air defense missions. They turned in their F-4 Phantoms for ADF F-16s during September of 1990. (Ted Carlson)

The two solo pilots (Nos 5 and 6) of the USAF Thunderbirds Flight Demonstration Team make a mirror image pass with their F-16As.

An F-16C of the 363rd Tactical Fighter Wing. The Viper was named *HAMMER TIME* and carried the markings of the wing commander's aircraft.

The F-16C of the 388th TFW was armed with 1,000 pound bombs. Crews usually applied chalked sayings to the bombs carried by the F-16s during Operation DESERT STORM.

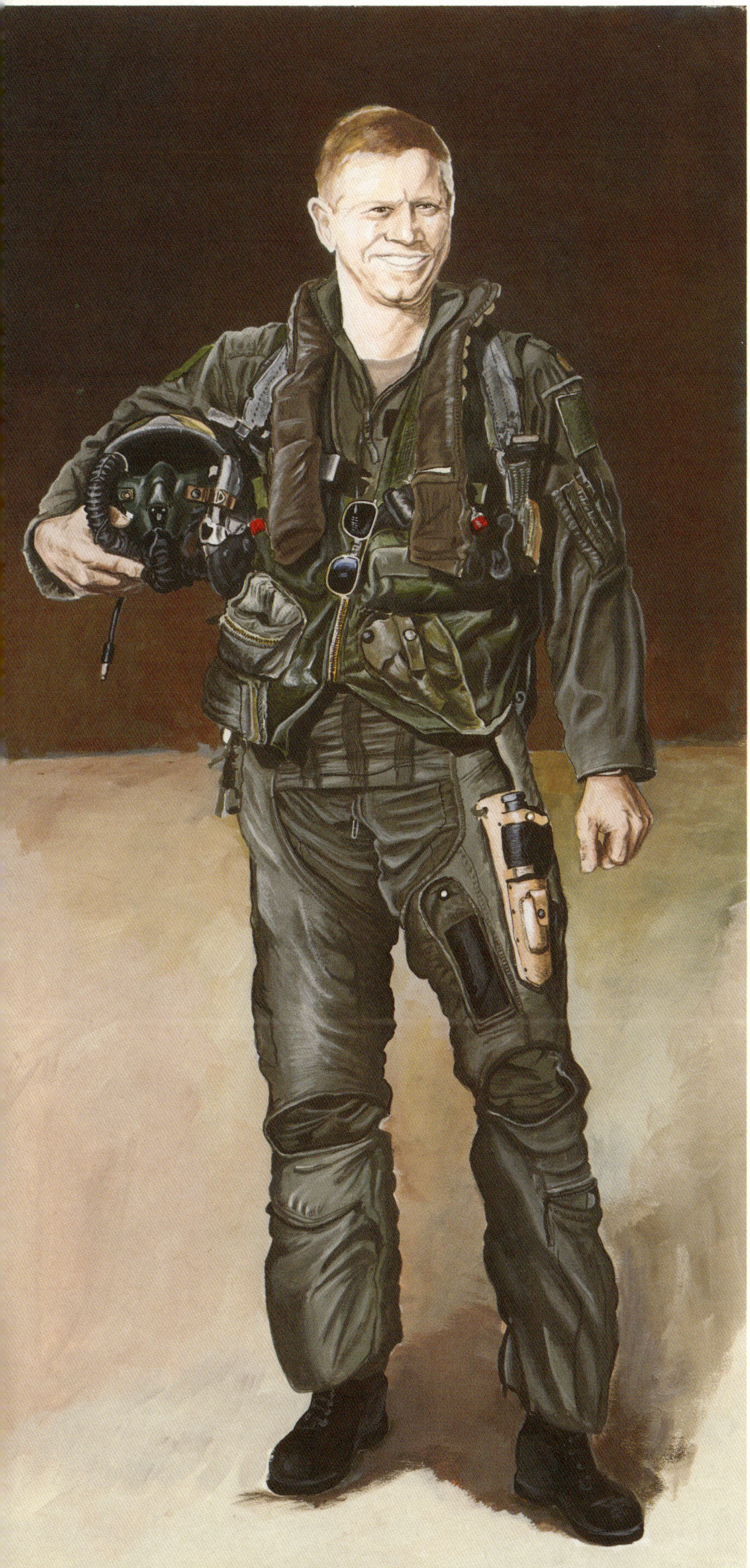

MAJ Bobby Armour flew with the 363rd Tactical Fighter Wing during Operation DESERT STORM.

Desert Storm Tails:
138th TFS
(Syracuse, N.Y.)

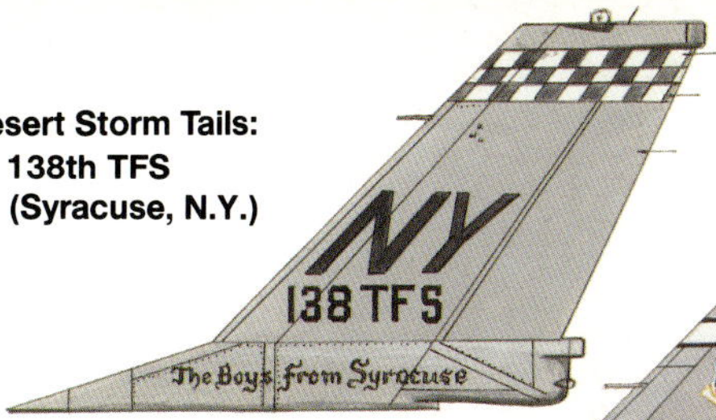

347th TFW (Moody AFB, Ga.)

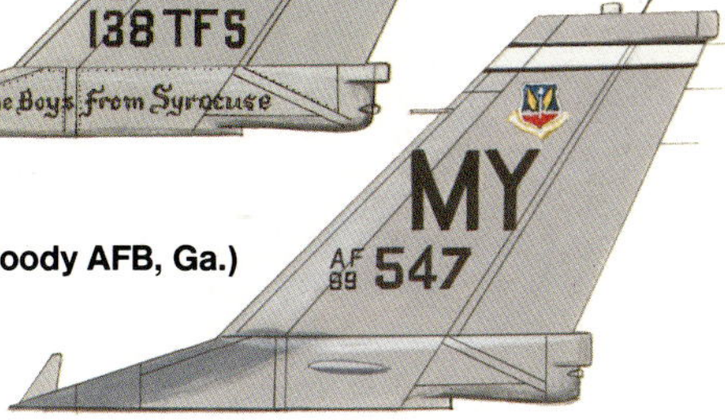

401st TFW
(Torrejon AB, Spain)

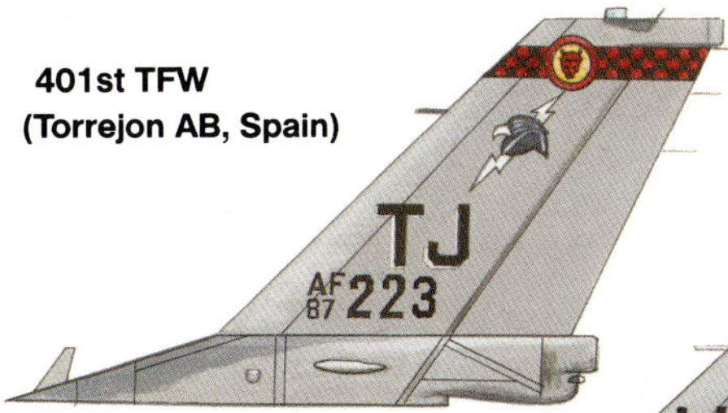

50th TFW (Hahn AB, Germany
- flew with 401st TFW)

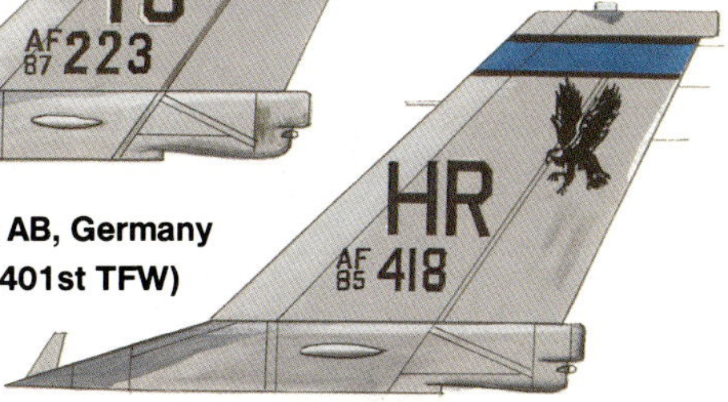

388th TFW (Hill AFB, Utah)

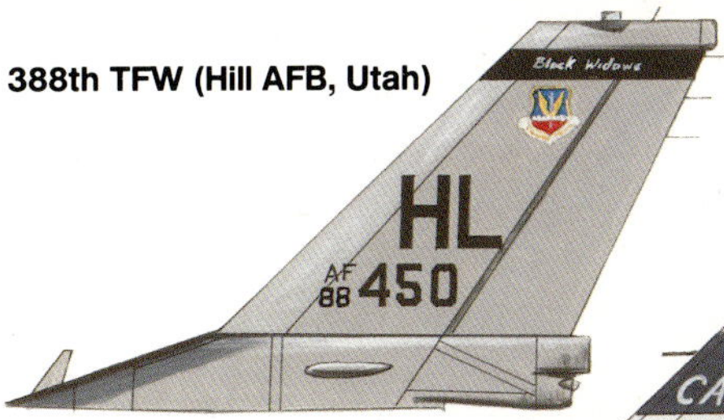

157th TFS (McEntire ANGB, S.C.)

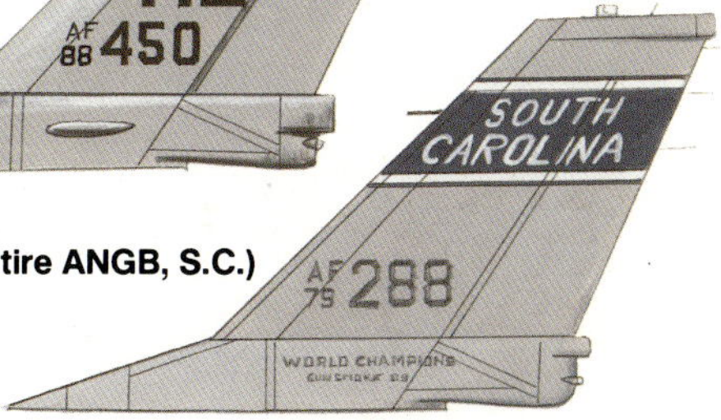

Israeli F-16C

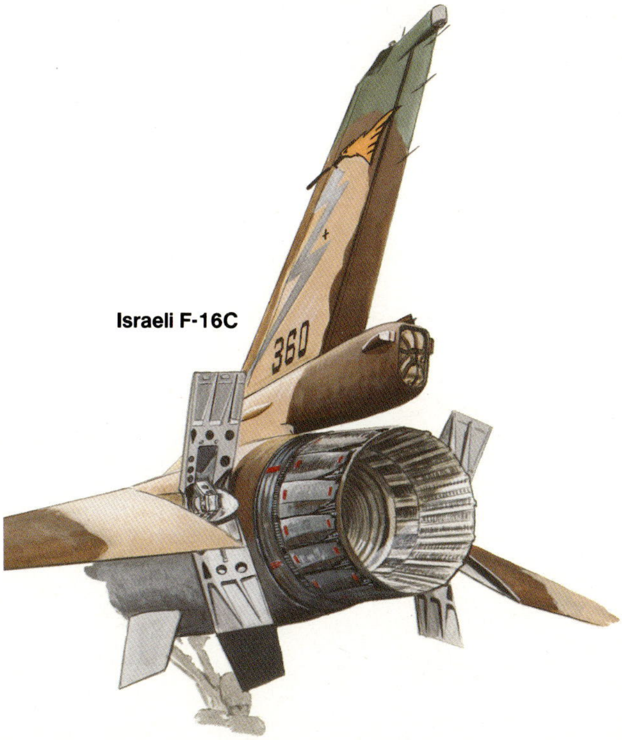

The first Air Defense Fighter-modified F-16 was this F-16B (82-0041) assigned to the 114th TFTS. A 150,000 candle-power night identification spotlight is mounted on the port side of the nose. F-16B ADF versions do not have the advanced IFF or HF radios which identify F-16A ADF versions, though all ADF versions carry the spotlight. (General Dynamics)

This F-16A (79-0403) of the 138th TFS, 174th TFW (The Boys from Syracuse) specialize in the close air support mission. They are the only unit equipped with the 30MM GPU-8/A gun pod which is mounted on the centerline station of their F-16As. (General Dynamics)

The 120th Fighter Interceptor Group of the Montana Air National Guard turned in their Convair F-106 Delta Darts for ADF variants of the F-16A during June of 1987. (General Dynamics)

An F-16A 80-0577 of the 182nd TFS, 149th TFG, Texas ANG on the ramp at Kelly Field, San Antonio, Texas. The 182nd was the first F-16 ANG unit in Texas receiving its first F-16s during 1986. (Brian Rogers via David F. Brown)

The 170th TFS, 183rd TFG of the Illinois ANG turned in their F-4Ds for F-16s in late 1989. The fin flashes sport the Blue and Orange colors of the "Fighting Illini" (the University of Illinois sports teams). (Bob Pfannnenschmidt)

An F-16A (78-0065) of the 466th TFS, 419th TFG Diamondbacks, Air Force Reserve (AFRES) on final approach for landing at Nellis AFB on 8 May 1991 during a Red Flag exercise. The aircraft carries an ECM pod on the centerline station. (Ted Carlson)

The 184th TFG, Kansas Air National Guard operates three squadrons of F-16s from McConnell AFB. The Kansas Jayhawks 161st TFTS was the first to fly the F-16, followed by the 177th TFTS and the 127th TFS. (David F. Brown)

An F-16A ADF of the 194th FIS, 144th TFG, California Air Guard shares the ramp at NAS Miramar, California with a Grumman EA-6B Prowler on 18 August 1991. The aircraft carries dummy AIM-9 Sidewinders, a centerline fuel tank and travel pods. (Ted Carlson)

This F-16C of the 614th TFS Lucky Devils, 401st TFW, is armed with two 1,000 pound bombs on the inboard wing stations and an ECM pod on the centerline station. Early in DESERT STORM it was thought that the F-16s might encounter a heavy air-to-air threat so they carried four AIM-9 Sidewinder missiles.

This F-16C was flown by CAPT Phil Ruhlman during Operation DESERT STORM.

An F-16N (BuNo 163573) of VF-45, NAS Key West, Florida on the ramp at Shaw AFB, S.C. on 11 March 1988. The Navy bought twenty-six F-16Ns to serve as adversary aircraft, four of which are two seaters. The F-16N is basically an F-16C with the F-110 engine, strengthened wings, deleted gun and an APG-66 radar in place of the APG-68. The aircraft are operated by VF-43, VF-45, VF-126 and the Fighter Weapons School (Top Gun). (Norm Taylor)

A formation flight of F-16s from the original five nations that purchased the F-16 (from the top) the Netherlands, USAF, Belgium, Denmark and Norway. (General Dynamics)

This F-16C (89-2037) of the 51st Tactical Fighter Wing at Osan Air Base, Korea during May of 1991, carries the markings of the Commander of the 7th Air Force, LTGEN Ronald R. Fogleman. (Paul Hunt via Norm Taylor)

A USAF F-16C in the MiG-23 Aggressor paint scheme. USAF adversary F-16s are painted in MiG-23 and MiG-29 camouflage colors. The MiG-23 scheme is a Dark Green, Tan and Sand wraparound scheme. (General Dynamics)

Norway has purchased a total of seventy-eight F-16A/Bs, manufactured in the Fokker Plant. This F-16A-10-CF (78-0290) is from No 332 Squadron, the first Norwegian unit to fly the F-16. Other Norwegian F-16 squadrons are Nos 331 and 334 at Bodo and No 338 at Orland. Norway's F-16s were the first to incorporate the drag chute housing at the base of the tail. (Norm Taylor)

An F-16A of No 350 Squadron, No 1 Wing, Belgian Air Force (*Force Aerienne Belge/Belgische Luchtmacht*). No 1 Wing is stationed at Beauvechain and it also includes No 349 Squadron (*Escadrille/Smaldeel*). (Dimitri Verdoodt)

The No 2 Wing of the Belgian Air Force is based at Florennes with two F-16 squadrons, Nos 1 and 2 *Smaldee/Escadrille*. No 1 Squadron's markings are Black, as is the thistle on the fin. No 2 Squadron's fin band is Blue and the fin marking is a Red shooting star. No 10 Wing, at Kleine-Brogel, also operates F-16s. Belgium bought a total of 160 F-16A/Bs. (Dimitri Verdoodt)

An F-16-5-CF (78-0248/J-248) of No 323 Squadron, Royal Netherlands Air Force (*Koninklijke Luchtmacht*), based at Leeuwarden on the ramp at RAF Brawdy, England, during August of 1985. Other Dutch squadrons include Nos 306, 311 and 312 at Volkel, 313 and 315 at Twenthe, 314 at Gilze-Rijen and 322 at Leeuwarden. (P. Camp via Norm Taylor)

This F-16A of No 31 Squadron, Belgian Air Force on the ramp at Nellis AFB on 22 June 1988 is configured with fuel tanks on the inboard and centerline pylons. (Brian Rogers via David F. Brown)

Armed with AIM-9 Sidewinders and carrying an external fuel tank on the centerline station, a Norwegian Air Force F-16A intercepts a Soviet Backfire bomber over the North Sea. Air defense is one of the primary missions of the Norwegian F-16 force. (General Dynamics)

A pair of F-16s of No 350 Squadron, Belgian Air Force fly formation with a pair of Mirage 2000s of *Escadrille Des Cigognes*, French Air Force. (Dimitri Verdoodt)

An F-16B of the Royal Danish Air Force (*Kongelige Danske Flyvevaaben*). Denmark bought a total of seventy F-16s: fifty-four F-16As and sixteen F-16Bs. They are operated by *Eskadrilles* 723 and 726 at Aalborg and *Eskadrilles* 727 and 730 at Skrydstrup. (General Dynamics)

Grupo Aereo de Caza No 16, Fuerza Aerea Venezolana (Venezuelan Air Force) has two squadrons of F-16s, No 161 and 162. Venezuela's twenty-four F-16s replaced Mirage III and V fighters in both the air defense and ground attack roles. (General Dynamics)

Indonesia bought twelve F-16A/Bs for the TNI-AU (*Tentara Nasional Indonesia-Angatan Udara*). The F-16s which are based at Ishwahyudi Air Base on the island of Java. They are camouflaged in a two-tone Blue and Gray camouflage. (General Dynamics)

Bahrain bought twelve F-16Cs and F-16Ds under the Peace Crown program. The first aircraft were delivered during March of 1990. The aircraft numbers and force legend on the fuselage side is in both English and Arabic. (General Dynamics)

Thailand has purchased a total of fourteen F-16As and four F-16Bs to counter the threat of Vietnamese MiGs. The aircraft carry a very small roundel on the fuselage side just behind the cockpit. (General Dynamics)

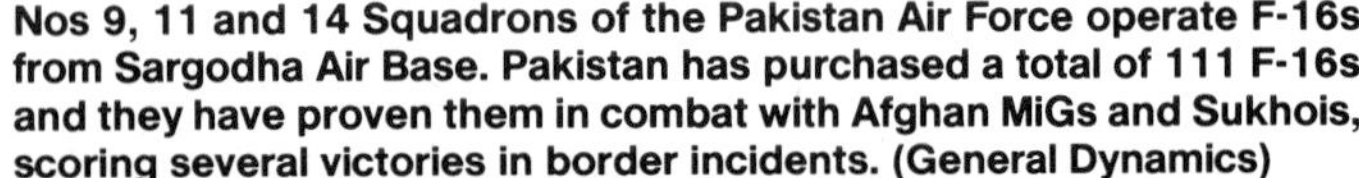

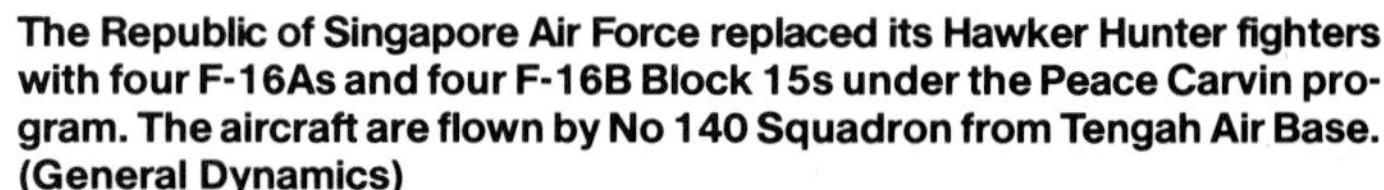

Nos 9, 11 and 14 Squadrons of the Pakistan Air Force operate F-16s from Sargodha Air Base. Pakistan has purchased a total of 111 F-16s and they have proven them in combat with Afghan MiGs and Sukhois, scoring several victories in border incidents. (General Dynamics)

The Republic of Singapore Air Force replaced its Hawker Hunter fighters with four F-16As and four F-16B Block 15s under the Peace Carvin program. The aircraft are flown by No 140 Squadron from Tengah Air Base. (General Dynamics)

An F-16C of the 614th TFS, 401st TFW leads a formation of aircraft based at Doha, Qatar during DESERT SHIELD/DESERT STORM. They include a Mirage F-1C of EC 12, French AF; a CF-18 Hornet of the RCAF; a Mirage F-1EDA of 7 Squadron and an Alfa Jet of the Qatari Air Force. (USAF)

CAPT Phil Ruhlman

The Red River Valley Fighter Pilots Association was founded during the Vietnam War. Membership was restricted to those pilots who had flown into the hell of the Hanoi/Haiphong complex of anti-aircraft defenses, which were the most intense in the history of aerial warfare. At first, the "River Rats" (as they called themselves) banded together as a mutual aid society. They were getting precious little support from Washington and very poor strategic and/or tactical advice, so several of the combat leaders, including COL "Scrappy" Johnson and COL Robin Olds, decided to host a series of "tactics conferences." These informal get-togethers were conceived as a method of integrating the air war a little more efficiently. They turned out to be much more.

When fighter pilots get together, the activity is likely to be intense, on the job or off. When it was time for fun, they worked hard at having fun, and through a sharing of one of the toughest assignments ever given to any military organization, a lifetime of friendships developed. The tactics conferences became reunions. Not "real" reunions, of course...the "real" reunions would have to await the end of the war. The get togethers at various bases in Southeast Asia were practice reunions. When the war ended with the release of the POWs, industrialist and patriot Ross Perot funded the first real reunion in Las Vegas. It was the party to end all parties. All POWs were welcomed into the River Rats. There were many toasts to comrades not present, and an undying loyalty to those who did not return resulted in the formation of the River Rat Scholarship Fund.

The River Rats have not only survived, they have flourished on the dual missions of supporting the families of those who did not return with love and with educational aid to their children and by reminding successive generations of military leaders of the mistakes that were made in fighting the Vietnam War. The River Rats dedicated themselves to the proposition that Americans should never again have to fight in a war we did not intend to win. Many of the junior members of the River Rats remained in the military and became senior commanders. They did not forget the mission. DESERT STORM was quick and deadly...all of the "never agains" of Vietnam were avoided, and the result was a stunning victory over the largest military power in the middle east. DESERT STORM has produced its own generation of River Rats. The river is not the Red River, it...or they...are the Tigris and Euphrates, but the spirit is the same, and all those aircrew who flew missions over Iraq or Kuwait were made eligible for membership. DESERT STORM River Rat #1 is CAPT Phil Ruhlman, who flew F-16s with the 401st TFW during the Gulf War. Phil, who graduated from the Air Force Academy, flew the O-2 as a FAC for 900 hours before going to the F-16. Shortly after the war, he wrote the following letter to the River Rats:

Eleven years ago, on the day that I graduated from the Air Force Academy, the keynote speaker (I can't recall who he was) said something very prophetic to my class. He told us that our generation of officers would be the next to see combat. As a matter

A "River Rats" patch of the Red River Valley Fighter Pilots Association.

of fact, he said that it would probably occur within ten years. Well, he was quite correct, and I couldn't help recalling his words the morning I flew my first combat mission during DESERT STORM.

My package of F-16Cs took off from Doha, Qatar, early on the morning of 17 January 1991. Our mission was the first daylight attack against Iraqi forces in Kuwait. Earlier, before dawn, the war had begun with deadly accuracy by fellow night flyers in "Varks," "Mudhens" and "Roaches," while "Eagle Drivers" flew cover. The "Hogs" and "Nails" were standing by to chew up the border in the early dawn. "Ponca" (AWACS) had the big picture with the air threat while the tankers (God bless 'em) were all on time and full of gas.

So there I was, ready to execute exactly what I had trained years to do. As I cruised up north, I realized that this was going to be a different war than Vietnam. (Don't get me wrong-you are

CAPT Phil Ruhlman poses alongside his F-16C "Viper" before beginning another DESERT STORM mission. His aircraft is loaded with Cluster Bomb Units (CBUs) and AIM-9 Sidewinder missiles. (Phil Ruhlman)

These "safe-conduct" passes were dropped on Iraqi troops urging them to surrender.

not about to read a dissertation by some young whipper-snapper on how he did it better. Hang on my wing, I think you'll like what I have to say.)

First off, I had always been quite pissed off by the fact that the politicians had so much to do with the air war in 'Nam. Picking targets, dictating tactics, restricting the "flexibility" of airpower. My heroes were the jocks who flew the "Thud," the "Misty," the "Raven," and got the job done amidst all the B.S., college protests, and bureaucratic who-ha. Good guys gave their lives for me. Now it was my turn to repay them, to set things right, if only my little contribution.

From the start, we knew this was going to be a different war. Everything seemed to flow. Everything had a purpose and there was little, if any, confusion on the overall plan. Interestingly enough, DESERT STORM was being led by the Generals and Colonels who were the young "butter bar" LTs back in Southeast Asia. Now, twenty years later, in Southwest Asia they were not going to let that war happen again. And today's politicians? Well, twenty years ago they were the young college students in the Poli-Sci course analyzing what was wrong with Vietnam. They weren't going to let it happen again, either. For goodness sake, even our President was an ex-Navy attack pilot!!!

The country was different, too. Out of the quagmire of the aborted Iranian hostage rescue, a new awareness and nationalism seemed to have taken hold. The Libya raid proved our resolve, Grenada taught us how to work together and Panama signaled a definite "Don't mess with us" attitude. Was it "Rambo," "Top Gun," and Lee Greenwood's "Proud to be an American," that did it? Maybe. Maybe it was also a need for a catharsis to rid ourselves of some deep burden buried inside for so long. Well, I'll leave that for the head-shrinks. Let's just say, it was time to set the record straight about the potential of modern airpower.

We also weren't alone. Over thirty countries stood united in their resolve to oust the Madman from Kuwait. We were a team. The issue was blatantly black and white, right and wrong, good versus evil. There was no doubt in my mind. On 17 January I knew what I was about to do was right. There was no doubt in my crew chief's mind either. Yeah, the 18-year-old kid who had never been TDY in his life, much less visited an Arab country, was busting his butt to launch my jet. The kid left Momma, MTV, and 7-11 behind, and was anxious for his "Viper" to score direct hits in Kuwait.

As our armada of fighters approached Kuwait, the radio crackled as scores of fighters checked in. Among all the callsigns, all the unique accents, everybody had that calm, cool, collected tone. This was it, the big one, the "Superbowl" and I was as ready as I would ever be. I thought of the two cardinal fighter pilot rules: "Speed is life" and "Check Six." Although the machines and tactics have changed, those eternal laws still prevail. As I flipped the master arm switch on, and went across the fence, it all seemed like a dream.

Nothing can ever describe the exhilaration of that first taste of combat. Nothing can ever describe the stark sense of terror as that SA-2 lights up your RHAW scope and won't let go. Then again, nothing will ever describe the sense of relief when your Weasel buddy calls "Magnum" and the SA-2 site evaporates in a cloud of dust. (I still owe that guy a case of scotch!!!) Nothing can describe the sensations as you see flak coming up to kill you. And nothing feels as great as when you shack the target!

As I returned that first day, I realized I had finally accomplished what I had trained 11 years to do. I was happy, relieved that I was now a member of the brotherhood of warriors lucky enough to be called into battle. Many warriors, back in the States, never had the chance to do what I had done. However, they were the ones busting their butts pulling double-duty and night-shifts while I was away. They too, made it happen. They too, are the unsung heroes.

For the next month and a half I had the opportunity to fly 42 more combat missions. As a flight leader, I was allowed to make

my own decisions, and I had the freedom to execute as I saw tactically sound. My commanders gave me their confidence and support. The war was pure textbook - AFM 1-1, right out of Maxwell - "Centralized Control-Decentralized Execution."

Some things in our war were different than in 'Nam: Lantirn, CBU-87, GPS, the SA-6. Some things were the same: High Angle DB, four-ship integrity and AAA. We had our POWs and still have our MIAs. Also, our brothers who have gone before...

So, why did we win? Well, because it all came together and was done right. It was also done right because you guys taught us what to do. You guys were the ones in the bar on a Friday night telling us war stories about Route Pac 6. You guys were the ones with that solemn glimmer in your eyes as we toasted with water during dining ins. You guys were the ones who ensured we got the new technology and right jets to do the job. Here is a toast to you and a nickle on the grass!!!

It is an honor to be the first River Rat out of Desert Storm. The Tigris and Euphrates now have stories as does the Red River. The heritage is safe, and the brotherhood continues.

Check 6
Captain Phil Ruhlman

When I asked Phil Ruhlman if he would talk to me about his experiences with the F-16, he started with a briefing on the F-16 pilot's lexicon.

The 4th and 421st Tactical Fighter Squadrons of the 388th TFW, home based at Hill AFB, Utah flew their F-16s from Al Minhad, United Arab Emirates, during Operation DESERT STORM. This F-16C is armed with Rockeye CBUs and Sidewinder AAMs, and carries an ALQ-131 ECM pod on the centerline station. (USAF)

This F-16A-10-CF (79-0295) of the 157th TFS, South Carolina ANG was named *THIS DAWG CAN HUNT*, and it did exactly that during Operation DESERT STORM flying from Al Kharj Royal Saudi Air Force Base. (Norm Taylor)

Nicknames: "Viper" - By far the most commonly used within the F-16 community - The unofficial name. "Fighting Falcon" - The official name...never used by its pilots, unless in an official briefing. "Electric Jet" - Popular early name. Not used as much as "Viper." "Lawn Dart" - A trend, for a while, by other pilots not flying the F-16, it was used in the early years when there were several F-16 crashes. "Small Tail" - Block 1, 5, 10, and early 15 aircraft. The horizontal tail surface was smaller than later models. "Big Tail" - late block 15, 25, 30 and present. Larger tail surface. Designed to improve departure resistance and landing control authority. "Big Mouth" - Block 30 GE-100 engine jets. Intake was flared wider to increase airflow. All block 40 and 50 jets are also Big Mouth. "Black Nose" - Early block 1, 5, and 10 jets had black radomes. "Block..." - F-16 production was comprised of several blocks/modifications. (Within the A, B, C, D designations). "Block 1, 5, 10, 15" - F-16A/B avionics and software changes. "Block 15s, 15S2" - Major avionics update to the F-16A/B radar. "Block 15S2 OCU" - Operational capabilities upgrade. Modified F-16A/B to carry AIM-7 Sparrow AAM and used data cartridge loader (DTC). "Block 25" - First F-16C/D - Essentially a "new" aircraft with major differences, such as Multi Function Displays (MFD's). This aircraft was considerably heavier (around 800 pounds) in the nose. All Block 25s were later upgraded with Block 30 software. "Block 30" - The queen of the F-16C/D fleet. Big Mouth GE-100 engine with outstanding performance and excellent mix of avionics. AMRAAM capable. 1986 production had two chaff/flare cannisters. '87 and later production have four chaff/flare cannisters. "Block 40/42" - First LANTIRN capable F-16. Some F-16 squadrons have navigation pods and targeting pods as well as terrain following radar (TFR). "Block 50/52" - Latest production version fully HARM/AIM-120 AMRAAM capable.

Any block 30 to 52 F-16 with serial number ending in "0" denotes an airplane with the GE-100 or 129 engine. Serial numbers ending in "2" denotes a Pratt & Whitney engine (PW-200, 220, 229).

The F-16 has grown to be a fully "autonomous" fighter, capable of day/night air-to-air or air-to-ground ops, using sophisticated weapons like HARM, AMRAAM, LGBs, Nukes and conventional weapons. The F-16 radar is slightly less powerful than the F-15, but pilots feel that it is more user friendly and presents information better. Integration with AMRAAM and AIM-7 make it on a par with other radar-guided shooters (F-18, F-14, F-15). In individual air combat performance, the F-16 still will outperform any other fighter in a dogfight. Block 40 and on have modified "EEGS" gunsights, which allow unprecedented accuracy at greater ranges and aspects. In general, F-16s with

General Electric engines are superior to F-16s with Pratt & Whitney engines.

On peacetime air-to-air training missions, we carry one AIM-9 (captive) on station 1 or 9 (wingtips), one AIM-9/AMD pod/or ACMI pod on the other wingtip station. We usually do not carry any tanks. On air-to-ground missions, we carry two 370 gallon wing tanks, 1 SUU/1 TER with BDU-33 and the same missile configuration. LANTIRN jets carry 1 NAV and 1 Targeting pod, plus a captive Maverick missile. Peacetime missions are enhanced by the video tape recorder and the "simulate" switch. If no bombing range is available for practice ordnance delivery, any "target" can be "attacked" by a video assessed delivery. Parameters and pipper placement at pickle/release are assessed. Units overseas in unrestricted VFR training areas widely use this function during surface attack tactics (SAT) rides.

Air-to-air kill validation in peacetime is strictly controlled through squadron published kill criteria. This normally involves valid missile track time, simulated fly-out, radar lock, and proper number of gun frames on target once the pipper is "hot." (Bullets have a time of flight to target.) On the enhanced gunsight (EEGS), the radar will compute bullet time of flight and display a "BATR" on the target showing simulated bullet impact. (In the HUD)

My interview with Phil Ruhlman took place in November of 1991. The war had been over for eight months and Phil was now an instructor pilot at the F-16 RTU at Luke AFB, Arizona. He prefaced his remarks about the war with this comment:

We are beginning to get more and more of the F-16 DESERT STORM veterans as instructors in the RTU, so I get a broad sampling of the feeling from other F-16 units. Most of the F-16 community feels that we did not get enough press during DESERT STORM. Because we didn't have laser guided bombs (LGBs) or the cosmic video provided by Maverick missiles, which CNN was so fond of, we just sort of got passed over. The F-117, the F-111, the F-15E...all did a great job and they are in the limelight because of their video-producing capability. Press is so bad, in fact, that some A-10 guy wrote Air Force Magazine with the comment that A-10s had gotten two kills (gun kills on helicopters) but the F-16 got no kills! The A-10s did outstanding work close to the front, but when they went deep inside Iraq, where we did most of our work, they suffered severe losses. I have been in F-16s for seven years and have over 1,500 hours in all the models, and our philosophy is a lot different than that in the F-15 community. F-15 guys..."Ego Drivers" as they are known by some ...are pure air-to-air. They tend to focus their attention 50 miles in front of the airplane, intending to shoot someone in the face at twenty miles with their radar missile. F-16 guys pride themselves on being multi-role; give us a job and we'll get it done, whether it is dropping bombs or shooting down MiGs. Get us inside that radar missile envelope, and we can "shoot down" Eagles pretty regularly too! Even the training environment is different. In the F-15 RTU, it is "We are going to bust you out of here...if you're not good enough!" but in the F-16 RTU it is "We are going to make you better...we are going to graduate you!"

My squadron, the 614th TFS from Torrejon AB, Spain, deployed to the Gulf on 29 August 1990, from Torrejon AB, Spain. We were the first U.S. military force ever to visit Qatar and we arrived at Doha with twenty-four F-16s, after a seven hour flight from Spain. We were joined by three KC-10s which had carried all our stuff and the base itself was pretty bare. There were a couple of hangars for the Emir's airplanes and twelve Mirage F-1s of his air force. They had their own support facilities, but they didn't have the capacity to support us, so consequently we built a bare base from scratch. We put up 100 tents, a kitchen, chapel, rec center, full communications net, full security police force, two tanks, armored personnel carriers, and built a bomb dump with the capability to build up weapons. We had deployed carrying six AIM-9 missiles per jet because we didn't know what to expect in the way of an air-to-air threat. Most of the bombs were aboard ships, being transported from the States. Our first couple of nights there, we stayed in the Sheraton, which we all liked a lot!. But GEN Horner said, "No way...we are not going to have an incident like Beirut." He was referring to the Marine barracks terrorist attack, and the security situation was something to be concerned about, so we moved back to the International Airport. We got an officer's building with twenty-four rooms and that is where the pilots stayed during the war.

The initial war fighting mentality centered around low altitude ingress, pop-up attacks, and low altitude egress. However, the density and spread of the Iraqi Army did not allow for a defined FEBA/FLOT (Forward Edge of Battle Area/Forward-Line Of Troops). Basically, they were everywhere...all over Kuwait and Basra. Flat, sandy terrain provided no cover for low altitude ingress, but it did make for easy target acquisition.

The first units deployed to the Gulf began practicing high altitude dive bomb attacks. Assumptions were that the Wild Weasels would suppress SAMs and high altitude attacks would decrease AAA effectiveness. AAA ranged from small arms to 23мм, 57мм, 85мм, and 105мм. That required ingress at 20,000 feet or better. Our prewar (DESERT SHIELD) training involved extensive large package employment (16-20 F-16s) with sequential attacks from 45 degree dives. Typical release altitudes ranged from 17,000 to 8,000 feet. The F-16 is small, gray and cool. (Cool refers to infrared signature.) It was practically invisible at altitudes above 15,000 feet, on clear, bright, sunny days. High altitudes gave us better air-to-air radar coverage and fuel consumption and higher Mach numbers could be used on ingress.

Politically, there might have been some uncertainty about what was going to happen if Saddam did not vacate Kuwait, but we were prepared to fight from the first days of DESERT SHIELD. DESERT STORM was still in a 'concept stage' and was not fully planned until just prior to January 1991. I thought I would be back in Spain by October, but then the shuttle diplomacy began and we realized we were going to be there for Thanksgiving and Christmas...and we began to hope that we would be adopted by some of the American oil families in-country. We did expect terrorist attacks on Christmas and when that didn't happen, I fully expected Saddam to back down prior to the 15 January deadline. Of course, he didn't and on the afternoon of 16 January GEN Schwartzkopf sent his execute message down to the units.

DESERT SHIELD was the best training we had ever had. We were essentially deployed for seven months on the most massive Red Flag exercise you can imagine and we were ready to go to war. We had huge strike packages, which included F-16s, F-15s, Weasels, tankers, Tornados, Jaguars,...the French Air Force was there with their Mirage 2000 and they played enemy air for us...and we were stationed on a base with twelve Mirage F-1s from the Qatar Air Force. We fought one versus one

This "blood chit" promised a reward to anyone assisting an American pilot in returning to friendly forces.

basic fighter maneuvers (BFM), two versus two air combat tactics (ACT)...everything with those guys. We knew everything about the F-1 before going into the war. In the process, we trained them better than they could ever have hoped to be trained. In our first engagements, we "shot them down" rather easily, but they learned from the experiences and they got a lot better before the war started.

My wingman during the war was a brand-new Second Lieutenant, Michael 'Timmy' Sewell, who had joined the unit in August, right out of pilot training. He was the best wingman I ever had...just because the training environment during DESERT SHIELD was the best we had ever experienced.

The Canadians showed up, just before the war started, with eighteen F-18s to augment the air defense force in the Gulf, followed by the French AF with more Mirage F-1s. So there we were, on this international airport, which probably never saw more than two DC-10s a day during peacetime, with all these fighter squadrons which were flying practice missions every day. We did learn to work together. When the war started, we flew bombing missions and the F-18s flew CAP over the Gulf. F-16s conducted daylight raids on Baghdad. The 614th TFS conducted the first daylight raid on downtown Baghdad on 19 January 1991. We were later primarily used on second echelon reinforced targets - bridges, bunkers, airfields, factories, ammo dumps, communications, etc. The F-16 was also used on first echelon targets in Kuwait, including Artillery, SAM, and SCUD sites. GEN Horner described the F-16 as "The Workhorse" of the war...it did the baseline bombing, hauling the iron, day after day.

Going in, we knew that the only way to defeat an enemy was to keep their air force from flying and we went right for the throat at the beginning. Even though they knew what was coming, we hit them so hard and so fast on Day One that it was mass confusion for them from that day forward. During that first week, Iraq was lit up like Christmas...the Iraqis had everything on, and the

An F-16A-10-CF 79-0404, 138th TFS, 174th TFW, NY ANG armed with the General Electric GPU-5 30mm gun pod on the centerline station. This was the first operational use of the pod and problems with the gun limited its use to one day. The 174th was the prototype F-16 CAS unit, turning in their A-10s for F-16s in November of 1988. (Norm Taylor)

Wild Weasels were expending their HARMs quickly. Our Radar Homing And Warning (RHAW) gear was really lit up, but it was pretty evident that they did not understand what a HARM was. After about a week, they figured it out and would not turn the radars on. We did not carry HARMS, but some F-16s out of Turkey did and they were the first F-16s to fire HARMs in combat. We depended on the F-4G Wild Weasels, but once the Iraqis turned off the radars, they didn't have to escort us to the targets. Then the Weasels became 'watchdogs,' simply patrolling the target areas, daring the enemy to turn on a radar.

On the first morning of the war, I was deputy lead of a seventy ship package (including our sixteen F-16s) against suspected SCUD launch sites. My squadron commander, LCOL Bruce 'Orville' Wright, was overall package commander. This was my most exciting mission of the war. We had been assigned to hit several airfields in Kuwait. Our sixteen ship flight was part of a package of seventy multi-national aircraft going to this target area. We were each carrying two Mk 84 2,000 pound bombs. As we crossed the fence, five of the sixteen were below the minimum fuel we had agreed on for going to the target. The weather was bad, with cloud tops at 10,000 feet. Orville turned the five around and sent them home, but eleven of us pressed on. (Eight jets split to a second pre-planned target, while we pressed

on the first targets with only three remaining F-16s.) I was number two and, just as we got to the target, there was a black hole in the cloud deck and the target was right in the middle of it! The squadron commander rolled in and I rolled in right after him from 16,000 feet. We screamed down the chute, aiming for a SCUD missile storage area. There were missiles going everywhere. They were shooting SAMs with and without radar guidance. The adrenaline was really pumping! I pickled, and came off with nine Gs! My 500 knots was immediately converted to 400 knots and my RHAW lit up with an SA-2 at my dead six. I heard AWACS call, "SA-2 Active, western Kuwait!" I thought, "No kidding, he's on me!" I punched chaff, jinked right...it went away...came back to egress heading...he's on me again...no kidding! My airspeed is down to 350 knots and I'm thinking, "This is it, he's got me!" As you get slower, the tracking solution is easier for the missile and I really had a solid spike, right at my dead six. I've got twenty miles to go to the border, but the SA-2 is closing at supersonic speed and I am convinced that the war is over for me. It was time to punch the tanks off. There is a little plastic cover over the jettison button so that you don't accidentally punch them off. The crew chief had glazed it over with white glue to make it look pretty! I bruised my finger but the adrenaline rush got that button punched. The tanks came off the airplane, it was clean, and I started to accelerate. Right then, I hear a Weasel guy call, "Magnum two." The SA-2 is gone...just like that, and I am outta there!

This DESERT STORM veteran F-16A of the New York Air National Guard retained its mission scoreboard on the nosewheel door after the unit returned to its home base at Syracuse. (David F. Brown)

I called him up right after I landed and asked if he had taken out this SA-2. He said, "Yeah, I got it just as you were egressing. The HARM came off the rail, and instead of doing its usual climb to acquire the target, it went straight for that SA-2 site!" I still owe that guy a case of Scotch. I learned my lesson from that. I never came off another target with less than 450 knots.

Early in the war, 60 F-16s, along with EF-111s and F-4Gs went 'downtown.' Our squadron had sixteen jets at the tail end of this group, and we were tasked with bombing strategic targets in Baghdad. All this garbage about us hitting civilian targets was just that. That stuff you saw on CNN, where they took their cameras to these different bunkers to show that there was nothing military there...we talked to Qataris that had been there before the war and they told us, "Don't you believe it...there is military stuff in there!"

My squadron lost two airplanes on that one Baghdad mission. Aviation Week claimed that only the F-117 flew over Baghdad, but that just wasn't true. There were scores of F-16s which went downtown, including my squadron, which went downtown on that third afternoon...in broad daylight. The anti-aircraft fire was described to me as incredible and the SAMs were not just fired under radar control...they were also optically guided. I saw one video tape (shot through the F-16 HUD) which showed the pilot, MAJ Emmett "E.T." Tullia, evading twelve different SAMs! As he evades them, he is forced lower and lower and what appears to be mist in the video is actually clouds and clouds of AAA!

CAPT Mike "Cujo" Roberts and MAJ Jeff "Tico" Tice got shot down on that mission. Mike took a direct hit and punched out under heavy negative G. When I saw the film later, I thought he was a goner, but he landed right next to a gun pit and was captured immediately. Jeff Tice took a round in the tank and also lost oil pressure. He made it about halfway back to Saudi before he had to punch out. He was picked up by some Bedouins, who traded him to the Iraqis. We were told not to carry any pictures, money, credit cards, gold...anything they might be able to use against you if you were captured. Well, that was baloney. I carried gold bracelets, gold chains, pictures of my wife...whatever I thought would help me make a deal, as well as for luck. Tico thought the pictures of his family that he carried saved his life, because it humanized him in the eyes of his captors. Guys flew with a lot of interesting things...mostly for luck, but also to barter for their lives with. They commonly described it as their "magic."

Studies had been done on the weather to determine just when to launch DESERT STORM. It was decided mid-January was the time when the least chance of bad weather existed...so naturally, we had the worst weather in fourteen years on day

one!!! The numbers predicted were a twelve percent chance of less than 6,000 foot ceilings over the target area, but it was actually less than 6,000 feet thirty-eight percent of the time for the first two weeks of the war. So there we were, up at 25,000 feet, with clouds under us...and there is no way you are going to go down and fly around under a 6,000 foot overcast, silhouetted against the clouds for all those AAA gunners! The weather got a lot better during the middle two weeks of the war and that is when we began to "attrit" the enemy.

Once the war settled into its attrition phase, the missions went something like this: We would take off with a flight of four to eight aircraft, loaded with two Mk 84 2,000 pound bombs or CBUs. After dropping off the tanker, we would contact a fast FAC, who would be flying a LANTIRN-equipped F-16. He would divide his area into "kill boxes," east and west. We called them "Killer FACs" and their call sign was "Pointer," which was appropriate, since our call signs were all dogs. Initially, they were diseases, but we later changed them to dogs. We used "Fang, Wolf, Cujo, Tico, Snoopy, Setter, Collie, Pug, Lassie, Boxer, Doberman, Rabid, Hound, Beagle, Bulldog, Huskie, Pitbull, Mutt." We would be about 150 miles out when we contacted the FAC, and we would ask him to describe the targets, which might be a row of tanks, or a logistics site, giving us the coordinates in the clear. He would ask us for our time on target and we could tell him to the second by punching the coordinates into our inertial navigation system (INS). The FACs were like traffic cops, because we had waves and waves of flights coming into the Basra area, where the Republican Guards were holed up. There were twenty tanker tracks, and the F-16s used five or six of them to feed fighters into this area.

The FAC would ask what time we expected to get there, and we would, for example, tell him, "15 minutes," then he would ask another flight...if that guy said "10 minutes," he got first shot at that target. It was really easy to manage, because you had a bunch of fighter pilots up there keeping track of each other. It was very common to be working a target and have another four ship of F-16s working a target five miles away. The important thing was to see the target. We had come a long way to hit it and we wanted to take the time to positively identify the target...and see if there was anything else. We were at 20,000 feet, but Pointer knew the area cold, and he could pick out the targets pretty easy. At night, the infrared capability in their pods even allowed them to pick out the "hot" tank from a group of tanks on the ground. (The enemy often holed up in one tank to conserve fuel and the heat signature would tell you which one it was.) Obviously, those became priority targets for the night bombers.

We would come across the fence (border) very high (30,000 feet), almost supersonic, then drop down to 20,000 feet when we got into the target area. There would be a couple of F-4G Wild Weasels hanging around, "smoking a Lucky," just waiting to see if any radars came up...and none did. See, the Iraqis got so

Six aircraft of the 4th Tactical Fighter Wing (Provisional). The F-16s are from the 347th TFW, 174th TFW and 157th TFS. The F-15C is from Bitburg and the F-15E is from Seymour Johnson. The EF-111 Raven is from Mountain Home. The ANG F-16s operated from Al Kharj RSAB in Saudi Arabia. (USAF by SSGT Dean Wagner)

An F-16A-10-CF 79-0404, 138th TFS, 174th TFW, NY ANG armed with the General Electric GPU-5 30mm gun pod on the centerline station. This was the first operational use of the pod and problems with the gun limited its use to one day. The 174th was the prototype F-16 CAS unit, turning in their A-10s for F-16s in November of 1988. (Norm Taylor)

Wild Weasels were expending their HARMs quickly. Our Radar Homing And Warning (RHAW) gear was really lit up, but it was pretty evident that they did not understand what a HARM was. After about a week, they figured it out and would not turn the radars on. We did not carry HARMS, but some F-16s out of Turkey did and they were the first F-16s to fire HARMs in combat. We depended on the F-4G Wild Weasels, but once the Iraqis turned off the radars, they didn't have to escort us to the targets. Then the Weasels became 'watchdogs,' simply patrolling the target areas, daring the enemy to turn on a radar.

On the first morning of the war, I was deputy lead of a seventy ship package (including our sixteen F-16s) against sus pected SCUD launch sites. My squadron commander, LCOL Bruce 'Orville' Wright, was overall package commander. This was my most exciting mission of the war. We had been assigned to hit several airfields in Kuwait. Our sixteen ship flight was part of a package of seventy multi-national aircraft going to this target area. We were each carrying two Mk 84 2,000 pound bombs. As we crossed the fence, five of the sixteen were below the minimum fuel we had agreed on for going to the target. The weather was bad, with cloud tops at 10,000 feet. Orville turned the five around and sent them home, but eleven of us pressed on. (Eight jets split to a second pre-planned target, while we pressed on the first targets with only three remaining F-16s.) I was number two and, just as we got to the target, there was a black hole in the cloud deck and the target was right in the middle of it! The squadron commander rolled in and I rolled in right after him from 16,000 feet. We screamed down the chute, aiming for a SCUD missile storage area. There were missiles going everywhere. They were shooting SAMs with and without radar guidance. The adrenaline was really pumping! I pickled, and came off with nine Gs! My 500 knots was immediately converted to 400 knots and my RHAW lit up with an SA-2 at my dead six. I heard AWACS call, "SA-2 Active, western Kuwait!" I thought, "No kidding, he's on me!" I punched chaff, jinked right...it went away...came back to egress heading...he's on me again...no kidding! My airspeed is down to 350 knots and I'm thinking, "This is it, he's got me!" As you get slower, the tracking solution is easier for the missile and I really had a solid spike, right at my dead six. I've got twenty miles to go to the border, but the SA-2 is closing at supersonic speed and I am convinced that the war is over for me. It was time to punch the tanks off. There is a little plastic cover over the jettison button so that you don't accidentally punch them off. The crew chief had glazed it over with white glue to make it look pretty! I bruised my finger but the adrenaline rush got that button punched. The tanks came off the airplane, it was clean, and I started to accelerate. Right then, I hear a Weasel guy call, "Magnum two." The SA-2 is gone...just like that, and I am outta there!

This DESERT STORM veteran F-16A of the New York Air National Guard retained its mission scoreboard on the nosewheel door after the unit returned to its home base at Syracuse. (David F. Brown)

I called him up right after I landed and asked if he had taken out this SA-2. He said, "Yeah, I got it just as you were egressing. The HARM came off the rail, and instead of doing its usual climb to acquire the target, it went straight for that SA-2 site!" I still owe that guy a case of Scotch. I learned my lesson from that. I never came off another target with less than 450 knots.

Early in the war, 60 F-16s, along with EF-111s and F-4Gs went 'downtown.' Our squadron had sixteen jets at the tail end of this group, and we were tasked with bombing strategic targets in Baghdad. All this garbage about us hitting civilian targets was just that. That stuff you saw on CNN, where they took their cameras to these different bunkers to show that there was nothing military there...we talked to Qataris that had been there before the war and they told us, "Don't you believe it...there is military stuff in there!"

My squadron lost two airplanes on that one Baghdad mission. Aviation Week claimed that only the F-117 flew over Baghdad, but that just wasn't true. There were scores of F-16s which went downtown, including my squadron, which went downtown on that third afternoon...in broad daylight. The anti-aircraft fire was described to me as incredible and the SAMs were not just fired under radar control...they were also optically guided. I saw one video tape (shot through the F-16 HUD) which showed the pilot, MAJ Emmett "E.T." Tullia, evading twelve different SAMs! As he evades them, he is forced lower and lower and what appears to be mist in the video is actually clouds and clouds of AAA!

CAPT Mike "Cujo" Roberts and MAJ Jeff "Tico" Tice got shot down on that mission. Mike took a direct hit and punched out under heavy negative G. When I saw the film later, I thought he was a goner, but he landed right next to a gun pit and was captured immediately. Jeff Tice took a round in the tank and also lost oil pressure. He made it about halfway back to Saudi before he had to punch out. He was picked up by some Bedouins, who traded him to the Iraqis. We were told not to carry any pictures, money, credit cards, gold...anything they might be able to use against you if you were captured. Well, that was baloney. I carried gold bracelets, gold chains, pictures of my wife...whatever I thought would help me make a deal, as well as for luck. Tico thought the pictures of his family that he carried saved his life, because it humanized him in the eyes of his captors. Guys flew with a lot of interesting things...mostly for luck, but also to barter for their lives with. They commonly described it as their "magic."

Studies had been done on the weather to determine just when to launch DESERT STORM. It was decided mid-January was the time when the least chance of bad weather existed...so naturally, we had the worst weather in fourteen years on day

one!!! The numbers predicted were a twelve percent chance of less than 6,000 foot ceilings over the target area, but it was actually less than 6,000 feet thirty-eight percent of the time for the first two weeks of the war. So there we were, up at 25,000 feet, with clouds under us...and there is no way you are going to go down and fly around under a 6,000 foot overcast, silhouetted against the clouds for all those AAA gunners! The weather got a lot better during the middle two weeks of the war and that is when we began to "attrit" the enemy.

Once the war settled into its attrition phase, the missions went something like this: We would take off with a flight of four to eight aircraft, loaded with two Mk 84 2,000 pound bombs or CBUs. After dropping off the tanker, we would contact a fast FAC, who would be flying a LANTIRN-equipped F-16. He would divide his area into "kill boxes," east and west. We called them "Killer FACs" and their call sign was "Pointer," which was appropriate, since our call signs were all dogs. Initially, they were diseases, but we later changed them to dogs. We used "Fang, Wolf, Cujo, Tico, Snoopy, Setter, Collie, Pug, Lassie, Boxer, Doberman, Rabid, Hound, Beagle, Bulldog, Huskie, Pitbull, Mutt." We would be about 150 miles out when we contacted the FAC, and we would ask him to describe the targets, which might be a row of tanks, or a logistics site, giving us the coordinates in that area. He would ask us for our time on target and we could tell him to the second by punching the coordinates into our inertial navigation system (INS). The FACs were like traffic cops, because we had waves and waves of flights coming into the Basra area, where the Republican Guards were holed up. There were twenty tanker tracks, and the F-16s used five or six of them to feed fighters into this area.

The FAC would ask what time we expected to get there, and we would, for example, tell him, "15 minutes," then he would ask another flight...if that guy said "10 minutes," he got first shot at that target. It was really easy to manage, because you had a bunch of fighter pilots up there keeping track of each other. It was very common to be working a target and have another four ship of F-16s working a target five miles away. The important thing was to see the target. We had come a long way to hit it and we wanted to take the time to positively identify the target...and see if there was anything else. We were at 20,000 feet, but Pointer knew the area cold, and he could pick out the targets pretty easy. At night, the infrared capability in their pods even allowed them to pick out the "hot" tank from a group of tanks on the ground. (The enemy often holed up in one tank to conserve fuel and the heat signature would tell you which one it was.) Obviously, those became priority targets for the night bombers.

We would come across the fence (border) very high (30,000 feet), almost supersonic, then drop down to 20,000 feet when we got into the target area. There would be a couple of F-4G Wild Weasels hanging around, "smoking a Lucky," just waiting to see if any radars came up...and none did. See, the Iraqis got so

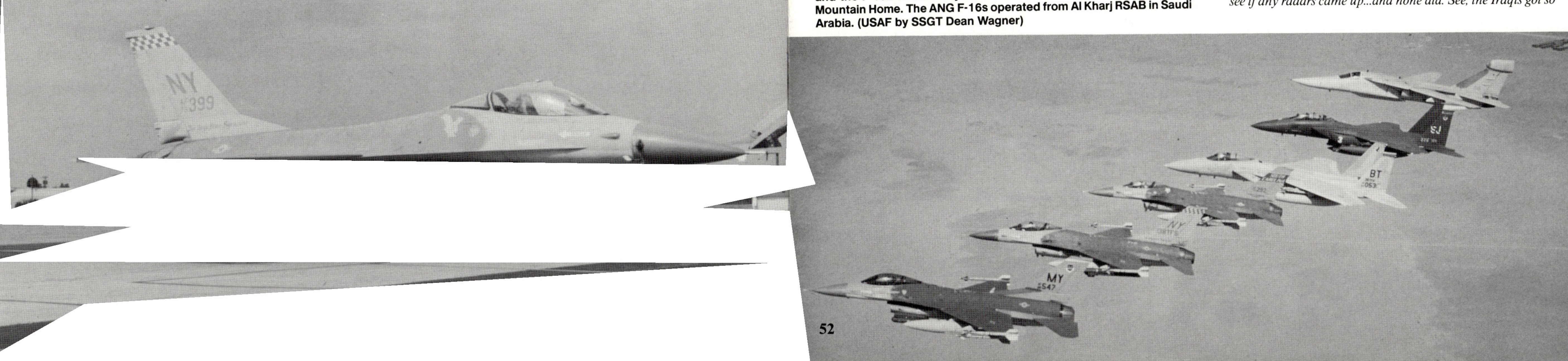

Six aircraft of the 4th Tactical Fighter Wing (Provisional). The F-16s are from the 347th TFW, 174th TFW and 157th TFS. The F-15C is from Bitburg and the F-15E is from Seymour Johnson. The EF-111 Raven is from Mountain Home. The ANG F-16s operated from Al Kharj RSAB in Saudi Arabia. (USAF by SSGT Dean Wagner)

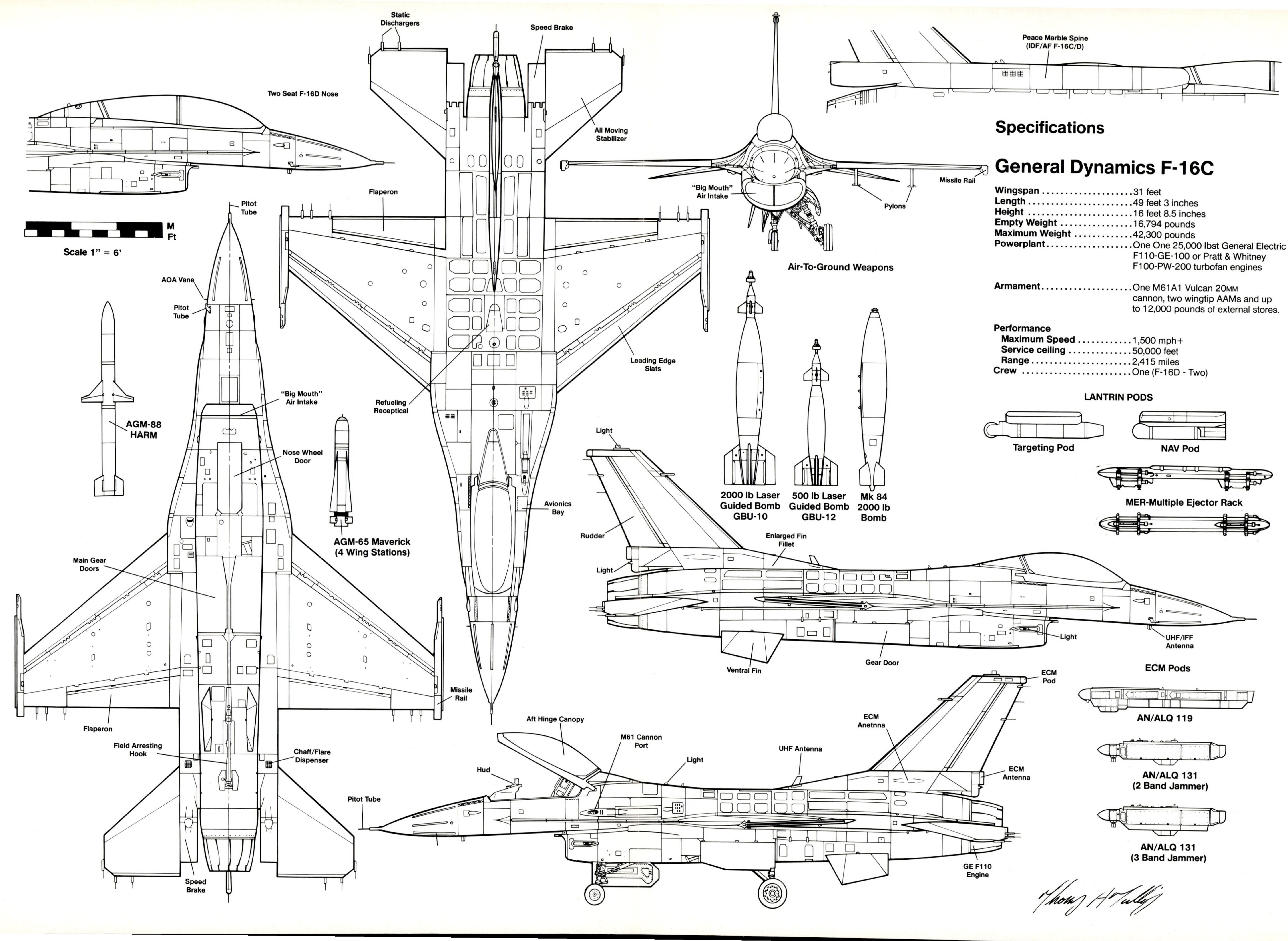

Specifications

General Dynamics F-16C

Wingspan ....31 feet
Length ....49 feet 3 inches
Height ....16 feet 8.5 inches
Empty Weight ....16,794 pounds
Maximum Weight ....42,300 pounds
Powerplant ....One One 25,000 lbst General Electric F110-GE-100 or Pratt & Whitney F100-PW-200 turbofan engines

Armament ....One M61A1 Vulcan 20MM cannon, two wingtip AAMs and up to 12,000 pounds of external stores.

Performance
  Maximum Speed ....1,500 mph+
  Service ceiling ....50,000 feet
  Range ....2,415 miles
  Crew ....One (F-16D - Two)

terrified of the Weasels that they would not turn the radars on. Coming across the fence, they might hit you with one strobe, just to try to pick out your altitude. But that was like trying to find someone in a dark room by turning on a flashlight for one second. You might get lucky, but then they are going to move and you are going to lose them again. So we came across at 30,000 feet, conscious of the SAM threat and always wary of a possible SAM firing. Our confidence was high in the Weasels, but we didn't get too cocky. The SA-6 was very deadly and it held our attention constantly. Still, we were high and out of the AAA. Once in the target area, we would descend to 20,000 feet. That made it easier to search for targets. AAA would come up, but it was optically guided, easy to avoid. Since the Weasels intimidated them, SAMs had very little chance of shooting us down. Our biggest threat was being seen by AAA gunners.

There were several tactics used. My favorite was to come into the target area with sections in five mile trail. The leader looks the target over...what is it? Do they see us? Are they shooting at us? He briefs the following sections and by the time the second section arrives in the target area, the leader's bombs are going off, making it easy for the trailers to pick out the target. When the environment was real permissive, we would take our time and make sure of our hits with multiple passes. At the beginning of the war, when they were still firing a lot of missiles, it was one pass and get out of there!

Our initial combat loads were two wing tanks, an ECM pod on the centerline (ALQ-131), and four AIM-9s (later reduced to two on the wingtips only). The gun was fully loaded with 510 rounds of 20MM HEI, although we never strafed. We carried a variety of bombs. Early in the war, we carried two Mk 84 low drag bombs with FMU-139 fuzes or two CBU-87s with FZU-39 fuzes, or two CBU-89s with FZU-39 fuzes. Later in the war, we carried four CBU-87s, or four CBU 58s, or four Rockeye, or six Mk 82 low drag, or four Mk 82 high drag (BSU-49s). The FMU-139 fuze malfunctioned early in the war, causing early detonation of the Mk 84 in flight. The 614th TFS lost one F-16 over Kuwait when the FMU-139 fuzed the bomb at release, almost blowing the wing off the jet. The pilot ejected and was picked up in the water by the Navy.

The scoreboard on F-16A (79-339) of the New York Air National Guard (the Boys from Syracuse) revealed an impressive tally of guns, radars, trucks, armored vehicles and troops. The aircraft flew at least seventy-seven missions during DESERT STORM (David F. Brown)

The older CBUs (58s and Rockeyes) were used extensively during the February Campaign. CBU-87 and 89 was saved until the Republican Guards pulled up stakes and bugged out of Kuwait. The CBU-58 and Rockeye was difficult to deliver at high altitude. The CBU-87 was a dream. F-16s also dropped a lot of leaflet bombs. We hated this stuff! It was dropped level with a timer fuze. F-16s would carry two of these bombs, called "whales," one under each wing. Sometimes, in a four ship, three jets would carry bombs, one would carry leaflets. Initially, chaff/flare loads were 60 chaff/30 flare for 87 year group F-16s. Later on, 90 chaff/15 flare was used. F-16As (and those with only two cannisters) carried 30 chaff/15 flare. Chaff was VITAL! (Authors note: Chaff consists of strips of foil which is ejected in "clouds" from cannisters to provide a false target to radar-guided SAMs. Flares are just that...and they provide a false target for heat-seeking SAMs.) F-16s from the New York Air Guard employed the GAU-8 30MM gun pod, but were not fond of it, since it was not as good as the internal 30MM gun in the A-10. Many block 40/42 Lantirn Jets employed IR Mavericks.

This F-16C (84-1212) of the 33rd TFS, 363rd TFW, based at Al Dhafra AB, UAE during DESERT SHIELD/DESERT STORM was given an experimental desert camouflage. It was so effective that on its first flight his wingman lost sight of him during the initial join-up! It was repainted in standard F-16 colors after a week of testing. (SSGT Wayne Argabright via Norm Taylor)

Sweet but Deadly was the name of this F-16C (83-0158) of the 33rd TFS Falcons during DESERT STORM. Warren Trask painted all the nose art carried on 363rd TFW F-16s. The aircraft has combat mission markings above the RESCUE arrow on the nose. (Norm Taylor)

In spite of the fact that we attacked them around the clock for nearly six weeks, there were still plenty of targets when the war ended. We should not have given them six months to build their defenses. You can build some really impressive logistical storage sites in that amount of time...and even to the south, there were artillery positions everywhere! The sand was just pock-marked with them. The trouble is, when you are rolling in from 15,000 feet, you are saying, "Is this really an artillery site, or just a bunch of junk?" So, if you got secondary explosions, you were happy, if not...well, you just didn't know, and there was no Ranger down there saying; "Nice hit." I flew forty missions. On ten of them, I got good secondary explosions. Ten were against strategic targets like power plants or buildings, ten were over the weather, using radar to drop the bombs, and on the other ten, I just didn't know if I was bombing a "real" target, or one that had been abandoned. Some of the missions were very satisfying. One day we bombed the telephone exchange which provided all the communications from the Iraqi General Staff down to Kuwait. Right after we landed, we turned on CNN and, sure enough, they were reporting that all communications with Kuwait had been lost!

On another mission, I was leading a flight of four against a bunker complex. I rolled in, dropped one Mk 84, pulled off and looked back just in time to see four trucks pull out onto the highway. I called my wingmen off the bunkers and told them to go for the trucks. Now, rolling in from 20,000 feet, the enemy is never going to see you...they just don't know you are there until the bombs go off. We were going to drop from 10,000 feet. The F-16 system is extremely accurate, but you still have 10,000 feet of winds to worry about, and we had discovered that a lot of the bombs were dropping short. One of the capabilities of the system is that it allows you to program changes and we told it to 'drop long,' and then started getting good hits. So, here we were, rolling in on a line of moving trucks and dropping from 10,000 feet. My bomb hit a couple of feet to the right of the cab of the lead truck, completely destroying it. The F-16 system is reasonably accurate from high altitude, as the normal high altitude CEP for the system is less than 75 feet. Now, if you have a tank buried up to the turret in sand, hitting ten feet away from the tank is not going to kill it, and that is why the F-15Es and F-111s used LGBs to kill the tanks (all Lantirn F-16s now have LGB capability).

A lot of our success in this war had to do with the attitude going in. We were told from day one, "No target is worth your ass." Point blank. "If it doesn't look right...go home. You have a

This F-16C (84-0257) was assigned to the 17th Tactical Fighter Squadron, "Hooters" during Operation DESERT STORM. This Viper was credited with fourteen combat missions. (David F. Brown)

This F-16D is carrying LANTRIN pods on the forward fuselage. Operation DESERT STORM was the operational debut for the LANTRIN system on the F-16 and both F-16Cs and F-16Ds carried the system into combat. (Texas Instruments)

twenty million dollar airplane there...and there is no target in Iraq worth you not coming home to Momma." The attitude was do it right, do it smart, if it ain't right, go home. In the Vietnam War, the targets were picked by Johnson from the White House. In this war, you had a CAPT in a Killer FAC picking the targets. His only instructions were, "Don't bomb civilian targets, don't bomb churches or mosques." ...and he would say; "O.K., that makes sense, I'm a college graduate...I can figure that out."

We did other innovative things too. On the fourth day of the war, the Iraqis had figured out what a HARM was, and they were beginning to shut down the radars whenever the Weasels were around. Trouble was, sometimes there weren't enough Weasels to cover all the bombers going in to Basra. The Weasel call signs were beers..."Coors," "Pabst," "Miller," etc. As we crossed the fence that day, I was leading an eight ship flight and we still didn't have our Weasels. I told my number five guy, CAPT Evan "Mai Tai" Mai, to act like a Weasel if they didn't show by the time we got to the target area...use all their terminology, call signs,...right in the clear, on a channel we knew the Iraqis monitored. (Authors note: In order to foil these listening posts, American fighters carried special radio equipment that broadcast on several different frequencies in spurts of limited time duration sequentially. Radios were preset to a given code so that the good guys could listen to each other, but the bad guys heard only milliseconds of transmission on any given frequency.) We were getting some RHAW indications and the Weasels had called to say they were going to be twenty minutes late. As we got to the target, we were lit up by an SA-6 site. Mai Tai called, "Fang, Coors, Magnum 6!" And the site turned off their radar immediately. (Magnum was the code word for the firing of a HARM missile. 6 indicated an SA-6 site.) Now, I'll admit my heart was in my mouth, because just two days previously, I had lost two buddies over Baghdad to these missiles.

As time went on though, the Weasels and the threat of the HARM really shut down the SAMs and all we had to worry about was the AAA. That was just like the old WWII movies. You would go driving into the target area and you would see these puffs of smoke. Some at 11,000 feet, some at 15,000 feet, some at 18,000 feet...all different colors. They never saw us, they were just firing at the sound, so we simply avoided the flak traps and attacked from different directions. And the key was to stay fast...come off the target with at least 450 knots of airspeed, using a 3 or 4 G pull. If you did get lit up by a SAM radar, move the airplane with a 2 G pull so you didn't degrade your airspeed.

When I flew with the wing commander, COL Jerry Nelson, who had flown combat in Vietnam, he was always supersonic going home, and even when he was on my wing, he would "pimp" me to keep the speed up. Since we hit the tanker just before going in, we came off the target pretty fat on gas and with a clean airplane it wasn't unusual to egress off target at 1.2 Mach. We would stay below the contrail level and when we hit the gulf we would slow down and climb. It was really funny......all these contrails starting right at the border and heading south!

No F-16s got any kills during the war, and that was the source of a lot of frustration. AWACs had the big picture and they would call any bandits in the air by referencing an agreed upon location ("Bullseye"). The location would be given a code name, so the call might be, "Two F-1s, 20 miles south of Pizza." Well, there were a lot of F-16 guys who were dying for a kill, and a call like that might draw a crowd. I was terrified of fratricide. During most of the war, there were no F-15s over Kuwait, so we were on our own as far as providing CAP, and if the chance had arisen to get a MiG during the attack phase, we would have jettisoned the bombs and gone right for the kill. We did have some missiles fired accidentally. You are trained to go to the air-to-air mode as you come off the target, which means flipping the thumb switch to "Dogfight." If you are pumping adrenaline and hold down the bomb pickle bomb as you switch to dogfight, there is the remote possibility that a missile will come off the rail. After the war, we were tasked with Combat Air Patrols, and we could shoot down anything except helicopters. We intercepted a lot of helicopters, but couldn't do anything except watch them. We did escort Saudi F-5s, Alpha Jets, and some friendly Mirage F-1s into Kuwait. You had to be real careful doing that, because the Iraqis had F-1s too, and the radar signature was distinctive. On one of these missions, I had a Navy F-14 roll in on us and go by me 200 feet away. I guess they were frustrated too...they only got two kills during the war. During the war the 614th TFS flew 1,300 sorties and dropped 1,837 tons of bombs. The cooperation among all the allies was outstanding. The Arab Coalition members felt that they were punishing an errant member of the family, and they really did their part. I was especially impressed with the professionalism of the Qatari Emiri Air Force (F-1s and Alpha Jets) with whom we flew several combined air strikes into Kuwait.*

The 1992 edition of the River Rats Reunion was held at the Sahara in Las Vegas. I was standing in the 100 degree heat on the hospitality lawn, (the room wasn't big enough to contain dozens of celebrating fighter pilots). I glanced up and there, strung across the facade of the top floor of the Sahara was a huge banner welcoming visitors to the DOHA, QATAR "fighter country," with the units stationed there during DESERT SHIELD/DESERT STORM named as hosts. The banner came back from DOHA with the returning 614th TFS. The feat of hanging it from the top floor of the Sahara demonstrated that while the weapons systems and tactics might change from war to war, fighter pilots do not. Phil Ruhlman and several of his squadron mates, along with DESERT STORM veterans of other units, fit right in with Vietnam Vets...they didn't have gray hair and they didn't have a tough time getting into their party suits, but it was obvious that the traditions of the River Rats were being passed to worthy custodians, completing the final chapter in the banishment of the "Vietnam Syndrome."

This F-16C (84-0240) of the 33rd Tactical Fighter Squadron was named *"Wild Thang"* and was flown by MAJ Bobby Armour (Now LTC). The protective cover over the nose radome was Blue. (David F. Brown)

MAJ Bobby Armour

Bobby Armour was one of the F-16 pilots who spent a very eventful few months in the Persian Gulf in 1990 and 1991. His account of those months and the missions he flew follows:

Our Wing (the 363rd FW, Shaw AFB, South Carolina) has a commitment in that part of the world, so we were primed to go when Iraq invaded Kuwait. At the time, I was TDY to Nellis AFB, Nevada, where I was helping to plan the wing's participation in a RED FLAG exercise in October. I was a flight commander in the 33rd TFS and shortly after the invasion I got a call from our OPS Officer, ordering me to return to Shaw. Within 48 hours of my return, we got the order to deploy to Al Dahfra, in the United Arab Emirates.

The deployment went pretty much as expected, following the

"Wild Thang" (F-16C 84-0240) of the 33rd TFS, 363rd TFW was the mount of MAJ Bobby Armour, who's name was carried on the port canopy rail. The joker had a Red hat, Yellow shirt, Green pantaloons with Red/Green pants. The lettering was Yellow with a thin Black outline. (Bobby Armour)

routes and procedures established in previous training exercises. We took off late in the afternoon and headed out over the Atlantic, with each of our F-16Cs loaded with three external fuel tanks, a travel pod, an ECM pod and four AIM-9 Sidewinder missiles. The late afternoon takeoff was by design, so the night portion of the flight would occur while we were still fresh. We rendezvoused with our tankers just off the east coast, and they stayed with us all the way to Saudi Arabia. The squadrons were comprised of twenty-four aircraft, arranged for this trip in cells of six. On the first day of the deployment (9 August), the 17th TFS got all twenty-four of their aircraft across. On the second day, my squadron got twenty aircraft across. One two-ship was diverted to Canada, and eventually returned to Shaw. The other two-ship was out of my cell and it was Squadron Commander LTC Ron Perkins' aircraft which developed a problem with the environmental control system (ECS). This happened during the night, just north of the Azores. His air conditioning system went full cold and, although he tried to tough it out, it was just too much of a problem to live with, so he diverted to Rota, Spain. (We divert as two ship flights to provide support for the aircraft having problems. Only two aircraft had problems.) I was the deputy lead, so I assumed the lead shortly before we passed the Strait of Gibralter at dawn.

As we flew down the Mediterranean towards Egypt, the adrenaline began to flow. We weren't at all sure that the Libyans might not take exception to our crossing their "Line of Death" and try to intercept the flight. The flight was uneventful and we turned right at the Nile, then left at Luxor, Egypt and proceeded across Saudi Arabia to the Gulf and Al Dhafra AB in the UAE.

The 17th TFS had arrived the day before and had sorted out some of the logistical details, making it easier on us when we landed. Ironically, the commander of the 17th, LCOL Billy Diehl and the Wing Director of Operations (DO) COL Van Sice also had problems with their ECS system and arrived with near frost bite. A lot of detailed planning went into making the sixteen hour flight possible. The tankers were always there and we always had enough gas to make a divert field. The Flight Surgeon issued 'whoopee cushions' to ease the strain on our backsides during the flight. We were not entirely unfamiliar with that part of the world, since our squadron had deployed to Jordan the previous June. We made that trip in two legs, so my longest previous flight in the aircraft was about eight hours. Once we got to Al Dahfra, one of our biggest concerns was having someone land gear-up, since we were all pretty tired by that time. We talked to each other the whole time and we were pretty fired up, so the flight itself didn't seem too bad. But after landing, when the canopy came open, the assault of 115 degree air was brutal! Most people assume that, since you are in the desert, the humidity is low, so the heat isn't as bad as it could be. Unfortunately, the humidity was in the 50% range, or greater, so it was unlike anything I had ever experienced and I have lived in Arizona and in the Southeastern United States.

Although the performance of the jets didn't seem to be affected too much by the high heat...that is, there was always plenty of runway available for what we had to do, the heat wasn't the only environmental factor we dealt with — the visibility certainly wasn't good VFR. The sun would be shining brightly, but because of the blowing sand and dust, you couldn't see more than a mile below 10,000 feet. We had the oldest operational F-16C models in the inventory and we were really pleasantly surprised at how well they held up under those conditions. We only lost one aircraft before the war started, and that was due to an in-flight engine fire.

As soon as we got to Al Dahfra, we went about the business of preparing for war and I really thought the war would start almost right away. The longer we stayed, the more action there was on the political front, and we began to think nothing would happen. We were among the first USAF bomb droppers to arrive, and we thought we would be interdicting the Iraqis as they came south through Saudi Arabia. Of course, had he done that, and considering his supply lines, we felt we could do a pretty good job of slowing him down.

While we waited, we began to put our arms around the problem of how to hit him and survive. It immediately became apparent that down low was not the place to be. There was just nothing to hide behind, and the AAA gunners would have a field day if we went screaming across the desert at low altitude. And being down low didn't give you any advantage when it came to spotting targets either. The blowing dust and sand made it easier to spot a target from 15,000 feet...looking straight down...than from a 1,000 feet of slant range. Of course, by the time the war started, visibility had improved because of the dynamics of winter air masses, but the AAA picture was still pretty grim so we decided to go to medium altitude.

The threat at medium altitude is the SA-2 and SA-3 SAM, but we felt the EF-111s and F-4Gs could deal with SAMs a lot better than we could contend with the AAA. Obviously, we were right about that! We made that decision very early, and we trained that way for six months before the war started. I think our confidence level going into the war was as high as you could

BLOOD STORM was an F-16C of the 363rd Tactical Fighter Wing. A high number of aircraft within the wing carried some sort of nose art. (Bobby Armour)

have hoped for it to be. At least once a week during this time we would put together thirty to forty ship packages of F-16s, combined with F-15 CAPs, F-4G Wild Weasels, EF-111 jammers, and all the tanker assets to pass gas to the strike force. We got used to what it took to get on and off the tanker, marshall, and head into and out of a target area.

We were strictly iron haulers. We didn't drop any precision munitions, and we didn't do any night attack. Our F-16s were not equipped with LANTIRN pods and we didn't have any Mavericks, so we left the night stuff to those guys who had the dedicated capability for night attack. We carried "dumb" bombs and CBUs, and we provided the mass of bomb tonnage that went up there.

On the first day of the war, I led the last eight ships of a package of 40 F-16s that attacked an airfield west of Baghdad. In addition to our bombers, we had a CAP of eight F-15s, four F-4G

The 363rd policy of allowing individual aircraft artwork spawned some great art and imaginative names such as *WILD CHILD.* **(Bobby Armour)**

HOOTERS STANDARDS was another F-16C of the 363rd TFW. Most of the F-16s had their art work applied in the same location on the fuselage. (Bobby Armour)

F-16Cs of the 4th Tactical Fighter Squadron, 388th Tactical Fighter Wing line the taxiway at Al Minhad Air Base, UAE. The second aircraft in the line carries the markings of the wing commander. (USAF)

Wild Weasels, two EF-111 Raven jammers, and five KC-10 tankers. The forty F-16s were divided into five eight ship groups. Mine was the last, and number forty developed aircraft trouble and had to abort, so we went in as a flight of three and four. Also represented in the 40 was the 10th TFS, which was detached from the 50th TFW at Hahn AB, Germany. They had joined us on the first of January, and became a part of the 363rd Provisional Wing. They had started a spin-up before they left Hahn and we finished it off with a thorough in-theater indoctrination. They worked hard to get up to speed, and by the time the war started they were pumped up and as ready as anyone.

We hit the target late in the day, and they weren't surprised. A couple of MiG-29s were capping the airfield, but AWACS was giving the F-15s good bogey dope on them from the time we stepped across the border and both were shot down by the Eagles when the lead F-16 was still ten miles out. The Fulcrums had started to run north, and the F-15s took AIM-7 shots as they pitched back south, probably at Beyond Visual Range (BVR). They were kind of surprised when the MiGs pitched back to the south and met the missiles head-on...they probably never knew what hit them. The first four Eagles got into the target area and got some SAMs shot at them before they hit bingo fuel and headed home. We still had four F-15s capping when we hit the target.

There were a lot of missiles fired that first day. We got a lot of RHAW and we could see the cons from all the missiles coming up. We also saw a lot of missile trails from HARMs off the Wild Weasels that were hitting the missile sites. I don't think the SAM sites had a lot of tracking shots, though they put a lot of missiles in the air. The weather wasn't very good in the target area, but it just so happened that our end of the airfield opened up about the time we got there. One of the eight ship groups had to drop through the undercast, using a radar delivery. Being the last guys to hit the target, by the time we rolled in there was a lot of flak. I had never seen it before, and as I rolled in I thought, "Golly, there's a cloud deck moving in here." But then I realized that that was not a cloud deck...that was flak! thirty-two F-16s had dropped their bombs before us, so the Iraqis knew they were under attack and they were really filling the sky with lead. They seemed to have more 37MM than anything else, and it was rapid fire AAA which we tried to stay above. That was our goal going

in...the really intense AAA was below 15,000 feet, so we were rolling in at 25,000 feet and dropping at 17,000 feet.

During our practices, we had worked real hard to put eight F-16s across a specific Distance Mean Point of Impact (DMPI) within 20 seconds. At the altitudes we were dropping, we knew that the bombs would be in the air about nineteen seconds, so we wanted the last guy to pickle his bombs before the leader's bombs hit the ground. That kept the target from being obscured by smoke and dust for those last guys. It also limited the exposure to AAA. We approached the target in a loose fluid four, then had number two slide over into echelon before rolling in simultaneously. When lead pulled off, he would delay his turn to the egress heading so the other guys could cut him off in the turn and get joined up in the same formation heading out of the target area. The first time we tried this maneuver, it wasn't pretty, but we had six months to get good at it and by the time the war started we could routinely put eight ships across a target in under twenty seconds. We each carried two Mk 84 2,000 pound bombs to hit the runways, taxiways, support facilities, and a few aircraft in the open.

As we egressed, we fully expected to get jumped by their Air Force. We had done a lot of training for this, knowing how you were going to split out of the package, how you would get back in after dealing with the threat. We were well prepared for an air-to-air threat, and my personal opinion is that the war would have been a whole lot different if the threat had been there. He did us a big favor by keeping his aircraft on the ground. We might have had more aces, but he could have disrupted the strike packages anyway.

The first week of the war we hit strategic targets, then we concentrated on the Republican Guards. The day-in, day-out stuff went to a specific area on the Iraq-Kuwait border. Occasionally we would get a deep interdiction type target in Northern or Western Iraq. These included Scud hunting and road or river recce. Eventually we deployed to King Khalid Military City, which was right on the Saudi-Kuwait border. From there we could haul four 2,000 pound bombs with one tanker rendezvous. Those sorties were shorter and we would go right back to KKMC, hot pit refuel and rearm and head back north. Normally, those four bombs would be dropped one at a time and our targets were dug-in tanks, bunkers, artillery positions, or supply dumps. We started off this campaign with specific targets, but progressed to a "kill box" tactic wherein we were assigned to targets of opportunity within a specific area. This resulted in a Fast FAC system, where an F-16, usually from Hill AFB (They had Global Position

System [GPS] equipped F-16s) would sit up there and look for targets, then act as a traffic cop when you got there. The Fast FAC really helped our effectiveness with the vast numbers of aircraft that were attacking the Iraqis. You just couldn't afford to sit up there and look for targets when you had guys coming into the same area right behind you.

Bobby Armour flew 119 hours in the war, averaging 3.5 hours per mission. The missions from KKMC averaged one hour, but some of the missions from Al Dahfra were as long as seven and a half hours, the average mission was four hours. In spite of the tremendous volume of missile and AAA fire, none of it came close to him. He feels that most of the missiles he saw were unguided, but also noted that, "the ones you see are not the ones you worry about." Several of the senior commanders in the 363rd had flown in Vietnam, and they talked about the differences between the wars. The leadership from GEN Horner (Commander 9th AF) on down through COL Huot, the wing commander, and COL Vansill, the wing DO, was great. They had ample latitude to get the job done as they thought best. The wing policy was that anyone...from the greenest lieutenant, to the most senior aviator...could advance any tactics idea he thought was worthy of consideration and it would be considered and adopted if it had merit. A lot of them did, and a lot of the tactics were changed. Lessons learned from Vietnam were remembered and acted upon. A lot of new lessons were learned and Bobby Armour's parting words to me were, "I hope we don't have to do this again, but if we do, I hope we don't forget what we learned...and we learned a bunch!"

Vipers of the 614th TFS, Lucky Devils search for enemy targets during Operation DESERT STORM. The wingman has already unloaded his CBUs, while the leader still has a 2,000 pound bomb on the outboard wing pylon. (USAF)

An F-16C Block 42 of the 69th TFS, which operated their LANTIRN-equipped Vipers from Al Minhad, UAE during DESERT STORM. The 69th used this capability during the rescue of CAPT Scott Thomas (33rd TFS). After he was shot down, four F-16s of the 69th located him and used their LANTIRN systems to locate and bomb Iraqis while guiding rescue forces to his position. (Ted Carlson)

This F-16C (84-0236) of the 17th Tactical Fighter Squadron carried an impressive combat mission scoreboard back to Shaw Air Force Base, SC after returning from duty in Saudi Arabia. (David F. Brown)

This F-16C (83-0145) was named *DEATH DEALER* and had a death angel character on the fuselage side. The aircraft is assigned to the 17th Tactical Fighter Squadron at Shaw AFB during the summer of 1991. (David F. Brown)

A little something from us to u
EAT THIS

HEY HERE'S
TO YOU!!

MAKING little HEROES

WHEN ASKING SOMEONE TO LEAVE, JUST
ISN'T ENOUGH... CONVINCE THEM IT'S
IN THEIR BEST INTEREST! YEA!

Just when you thought it
was safe 2000 II THE MOVIE!

THIS ONE'S FOR DIANE

YODIE, QUIT READING
BOMBS AND GET BACK TO
WORK!

SNAPPER
HEADS RULE

Pilots from the 614th Tactical Fighter Squadron Lucky Devils conduct a debriefing alongside their aircraft immediately following their first mission of the war on 17 January 1991. (USAF)

FOSTERS EXPRESS carried a Kangaroo and its child on the fuselage side. (Bobby Armour)

HOT COCK had a pair of young ladies to keep him company. (Bobby Armour)

WAR WENCH was another 363rd TFW F-16C. (Bobby Armour)

This F-16C carried the popular cartoon character the Tasmanian Devil armed with a Sidewinder missile. (Bobby Armour)

"CODE - ONE CANDY" was one of the best looking ladies to grace the side of an F-16. (Bobby Armour)

NEXT expressed the feelings of many F-16 pilots and ground crews. (Bobby Armour)

Eight F-16s wait their turn on the KC-135R after hitting targets in enemy territory. These were just a part of the vast air armada that attacked Iraqi positions in Kuwait and Iraq on a daily basis during Operation DESERT STORM. (USAF)

This Iraqi hardened aircraft shelter was not hard enough to withstand American 2,000 pound bombs dropped from F-16s. Not only was the shelter severely damaged, the aircraft inside were destroyed. (USAF)

A disabled Iraqi SA-6 Gainful Surface-to-Air Missile (SAM) transporter with a load of inoperable missiles. Just one of the many targets destroyed by F-16s in Iraq. (USAF)

Through his leadership and commitment to military control of Operation DESERT STORM, President George Bush contributed as much to the victory as if he had been in the cockpit...which he was during an earlier visit to General Dynamics' Fort Worth facility (while he was still Vice-President). (General Dynamics)